Rev. Marilee Ann

The Trilogy – Book I

ANCIENT WISDOM FOR NOW!
CRYSTALS
AND THE
13 CRYSTAL SKULLS

Rev. Marilee Ann Snyder-Nieciak

**Internationally Recognized Shamanic Practitioner,
Transformational Author and Crystal Skull Guardian sharing
ANCIENT WISDOM FOR NOW!**

To You, Dear Reader:

Thank you for joining me on my continuing two and a half year adventure as my companion and "seeker". I want to share what I have learned once I accepted my assignment from my Soul and Ancestors. I am continually expanding my awareness and consciousness by being here. This book is one of courage, learning, healing, teaching and growth. I was told a reference book, like a text book to teach with... I was given this assignment because of my transformational stories, enthusiasm and openness.

Know that each portion of this book stands alone with personal notes interspersed throughout. Read at your leisure.

First and foremost – I'm so excited that you are joining my adventure with the cutting edge technology of Shamanism that is 40,000 years old. There are threads in story and each chapter that touch each other. It is the weaving of a story that shows how the individual parts weave the fabric of wholeness. Hopefully it will demonstrate how we are all connected to each other and to the matrix of Earth and the Universe and Beyond to the Multi-verses...

After my "Death Experience" in 1972 I studied Ancient Healing Techniques because I *KNEW* there was more, more to know and different ways of living that honored the entirety of which we are. I founded Sage Spirit Terra in 1996. From 1991 to the present, I am always studying. I became a Reiki Master/Teacher and Dar'Shem III; Akashic Records Counselor and Teacher. I am a Certified Shamanic Practitioner of Ceremony and Ritual; Shamanic Journeys; Drum Circles; Soul Retrieval; Extraction and Divination. As, Rev. Marilee, I provide Spiritual Counseling and monthly New Moon Drum Circles. In 1996 Drum Circles began in a loft in Chicago's Chinatown to honor the Earth calendar; continuing to the present on the *"Healing Spirit Land"*. In 2002 I was awarded a Sacred Pipe and given my own Method of teaching the Akashic Records in alignment with each individual's vibration and frequency.

In 2001, I finally followed guidance regarding the Ancient Wisdom of Essential Oils and became a Young Living Essential Oils distributor # 431711 and I continue to use them my own benefit, my family, friends and with clients. In each bottle of pure essential oil is a bit of Source to heal your body, mind, emotions and to soothe your Soul and Spirit.

In 2003, I opened my Spiritual Healing Practice with the purchase of her Quantum Biofeedback machine. On January 31, 2007 I received my International Quantum Biofeedback Practitioner Certification.

Rev. Marilee graduated from Purdue University's Krannert School of Business in 1969. I am an entrepreneur. I opened my first business in Chicago as a Real Estate Broker in 1982.

We need to Share what we need to learn. In keeping with this tradition and of continual transformation, I was been guided to learn about the 13 Crystal Skulls with Akashic Records and Shamanic Journeys and to:

Share the Wisdom,
Share the Knowledge,
Share the Light,
Share the Love,
Share the Crystals and
Share the Original 13 Crystal Skulls.

My personal experience and belief is that Shamanism is a field of knowledge that continually expands. It is the first method of accessing our Akashic Records, the records of our Souls from inception, through to the present with the possibilities for our enfoldment.

It is August of 2013 and one year after I completed the first manuscript, we are revising and expanding the information and the pictures as we change our format from an e-book to a print.

When I accepted this assignment from my Soul and Ancestors, I was being given knowledge and wisdom that excited me and pushed me to learn more so that I could share it in drum circles and in this book and the ones to follow.

The knowledge and wisdom is presented differently in each part – So enjoy your Experiential Reading Adventure as you discover Crystals, Crystal

Skulls, Your Power Skull(s) and what works for you. Then there are the Skull Legends and The Information that each individual Skull wants you to have...

Shungo (My Heart to Your Heart), Marilee

Coming Soon – Book II and Book III

ANCIENT WISDOM for NOW! *Prayers and Guided Meditations*
ANCIENT WISDOM FOR NOW! *Healing Naturally with Shamanism, and Creator's Gift, Pure Therapeutic Grade Essential Oils*

Thank You with appreciation and gratitude to those people that helped get this book ready as an e-book and in print.

They are:

Cover Design and e-book formatting and uploading: Kimberly Burnham
Cover Photo: Bill Homann
Editing: Kathleen Jennings for e-book
Medicine Wheel Drawings: Deane Gemmell - The Saga-Oracle
Cover Design, print formatting and upload: Diane Nelson
Ancient Wisdom for Now Logo by Alex Strangius

For rights information contact:
https://www.ancientwisdomfornow.com
or mail request to:
Sage Spirit Terra, 9464 North Meer Road, Michigan City, IN 46360

ISBN-13: 978-0-9898570-0-0

*[Shamanism, Spirituality, New Age Crystals, Numerology,
Metaphysics, Healing and Skulls]*

TABLE OF CONTENTS

PART I

THE BEGINNING

INTRODUCTION:

Portions of the introduction can also be found before the Table of Contents because I want you to know why this book exists – it is for you, the reader! Because of my gifts that I didn't recognize or know existed, I have been led and guided each step by my helping Spirits. They have always served me without my realizing it or having any conscious awareness of the Light and Power around me.

From 1979 to mid-1982 I was traveling weekly for my job. I'd get on the airplane and nod out... Once we had reached our flying altitude, I'd wake up and have answers on how to the lease condominiums on the property I was visiting. Years later, when I was studying Shamanism, my mentor suggested that I had been going on journeys in the airplane for guidance from the Upper World. What do you think?

In the early 90's during my first Akashic Record Reading with a man in Alaska, I was told my enthusiasm was my greatest gift because that is how I shine my Light.

I didn't even know what that meant 20 years ago. So with much training, Remembering and experiential healing I arrived ready for the next odyssey – This book.

Why me, Marilee? I went on some Shamanic Journeys to help you the Reader and me understand and know why I was given this assignment to write and why I am writing this Trilogy.

My question to my guides and helpers – What is my purpose and what is my gift?

Your stories are your gift with your openness and your enthusiasm.

Your purpose is to share your stories of transformation and growth so that others, including you dear reader, can expand their conscious awareness of the other worlds and our connection to everything with your books, your online blogs along with your Ancient Wisdom for NOW radio and television shows, live presentations and classes.

Sharing is really important to me personally. Actually I love sharing, my home, my stories, my experiences, my wisdom and my knowledge to help people and myself...I share what I need to learn for myself and my Soul's growth.

NOW - I want to share the wisdom of the 13 Crystal Skulls by showing you how to access the Skulls and Crystals with Shamanic "journeys" and Numerology.

Let's start with the properties of Quartz Crystals...

CLEAR QUARTZ CRYSTAL:

You will soon figure out that I am an avid reader. In researching various bits and pieces of information to share, I discovered that I had most of the books in my Library. I have always loved Melody's book *"Love Is in the Earth"*. The title tells is all about clear *Quartz Crystal* – It is Love and Light.
The reference book I particularly like for this section is by Luc Bourgault. It is called *"The Native American Secrets of Crystal Healing"*. It is his teachings in the Native American way as he learned from a Tsalagi (Cherokee) Faith Healer, Elder and Leader named Dhyani Ywahoo and from Oh Shinnah Whitewolf of the Teneh (Apache).

This is important because these are the only two nations to provide chosen people with extensive training in prayer, meditation, healing and ceremony. They are also the only ones to develop the Therapeutic use of Crystals. In their way – the training is extensive before the student is allowed to touch the Crystals. This integrity of purpose and intention is important because of the knowledge and wisdom that crystals have, absorb and broadcast.

The Venerable Dhyani Ywahoo says that quartz crystal is NEITHER solid or liquid; it vibrates at 786,000 pulses per millisecond, its continuum moving faster than light, its vibration the axis of the Universe.

This was proven in experiments where a crystal stopped the light being sent to it for one minute. THEN THE BEAM OF LIGHT CONTINUED FLOW THROUGH THE CRYSTAL. THE ENTIRE ARTICLE WITH TECHNICAL DETAILS BY SEBASTIAN ANTHONY WAS PUBLISHED ON JULY 25, 2013 ON THE WEBSITE: http://www.ExtremeTech.com.

To work with clear crystals and polished Crystal Skulls we must first polish our own crystal.

Our brain has a pineal gland that connects us to the Universe and beyond including our own Soul. This gland begins turning to crystal at about age 18. If we do not work with our own crystal, working with others becomes difficult, so regardless of your faith or spirituality. Begin with groups and expand yourself with different teachings and healing modalities. The key is MEDITATION to hone and heal ourselves. We must learn to communicate with the unseen parts of ourselves (Spirit and Soul).

The next attribute of Love that is critical in all Spiritual work and when working with Crystals is RESPECT. We must respect Mother Earth as the Source of All Living Beings and Intelligences. She is their home as she is our home. The Crystals and Crystal Skulls are her children and must be treated with Respect and Care, not something that many humans from our Western Culture do well. The Earth is a Living, Intelligent Being who has passed all of this knowledge and wisdom to the crystal beings. The Crystal Skulls are the most advanced.

Once we Meditate and demonstrate our Respect by smudging with sacred herbs of Sage, Cedar, Sweetgrass with corn and tobacco offerings on the Alter Home we create for them. We must love and care for our Crystals and our homes by cleaning them energetically by smudging with Sage, Cedar and Sweetgrass.

If our crystals are new, we must clean them and reprogram them erasing any residual information that is not for their or our highest and best good. To clean the first time:

*Put in a natural container of glass, ceramic or clay with a teaspoon of Sea Salt per quart/liter of spring or distilled water. No metal that will absorb the energy and no plastic which is synthetic. It must be Sea Salt to remove the

3

improper ions and create the proper ionic field for the crystals. We remove the positive Ions (free radicals) and replace them with Negative Ions which help clean and clear with Love that which no longer serves us.

*Immerse the crystals or crystal Skulls for 7 days and 7 nights. Then run water over them. Every so often place them under running water for one or two hours.

Clear quartz crystal is alive and has extensive memory – that is why they are used for storage of information on computer chips and for healing. They help the body remember health. Because of this vast memory of where they have been, who has used them and their programming – it is imperative to properly clean them before using them for yourself. It is the molecular structure of quartz crystal that gives it these wonderful properties.

One of the properties of Quartz Crystal is its ability to dispel positive ions while releasing its negative ions. This is because Quartz Crystal is one of the most perfect physical forms in the Universe. This perfection allows it to act as a catalyst of our perfection, for deep down we are all perfect because we are from the Divine, who's Light we emanate. Crystal helps us brighten our Light.

Clear Quartz Crystal is pure Light. Although it appears solid it in fact vibrates with frequencies that far surpass our actual comprehension. It is one of the most perfect forms in the known Universe. From the Light and structural perfection flow Love, Intelligence, Knowledge, Wisdom on the beams of Light. To me crystals are Lighted Love.

It is this perfection of Structure with Lighted Love that allows us to receive information and guidance from the Original 13 Crystal Skulls. They have been gathering information to share for eons. The 13 Crystal Skulls have asked me to be one of the people to share their wisdom and information with you and help you find your Power Skull (In Part III)

The Time Is NOW!

WHY THIS PROJECT – SOURCE AND GUIDANCE?

In our conversation it is now time to explore *"Why the Original 13 Crystal Skulls?"* I was guided or invited by my Akashic Records (The Record of my Soul from inception to the present with the possibilities for enfoldment) to have the conversations with the 13 Crystal Skulls in numerical order of Skull 1 to 13.

You ask *"How did all this come about and how did you receive or find the information to write about the Original 13 Crystal Skulls?"*

My Information came by accessing Akashic Records and from the direct revelation received from each of the Skulls by using the Shamanic Journey Technique in my sessions. We use this technique in all of our drum circles and on our radio and TV programs. My friend and I each worked on our individual manuscripts, yet asked the same questions and receiving answers unique to our individual vibrations and frequencies. Our answers were different.

It all started on January 17, 2011 with an Akashic Record Reading much to my surprise and chagrin. Although I'd been told in an advanced Akashic Record class in 2000 that I'd write atleast one book, probably more. I am published in two other books as I write with more coming.

Some of our initial questions and answers are included so that you, our reader, can follow the procession that led to this book with additional experiences scattered along the way.

January 17, 2011 – QUESTIONS:

What do we need to know from the Skulls?

At one time in the far distant past you and Marlene were Keepers of the 13 Skulls.

How do we work with the 13 Skulls?
How do we bring the Wisdom of the Skulls forward?

The 13 Crystal Grandmothers have new information to come through regarding TRUTH, HEALING and TRANSFORMATION. You will work with the Skulls through the Akashic Records expanding Your Light, Love and Wisdom to work with the Beings of the Earth for Manifestation and Transformation.

You will be working with the 2nd Dimension – The Crystals of the Telluric Realm or the 2nd Dimension and the Transmutation of Viruses. The 13 Crystal Skulls are of Telluric Realm as Barbara Hand Clow identifies that part of the Earth between the Iron Crystal Core (which vibrates at a much higher rate than the Telluric Realm) and the Earth's Crust and the third Dimension where we live.

MORE QUESTIONS and ANSWERS from My AKASHIC RECORDS:

What is my relationship with the Telluric Realm (2-D)?

Your relationship with the Telluric Realm is deep. It is what you work with all of the time for truly the Stones and Bones hold the Records of the Earth. You have an affinity for Crystals and the Entire Telluric Realm with your SCIO (quantum biofeedback machine)

How Am I to work with the Telluric Realm (2-D)?

Through Shamanic Journeys to Mother Earth, viruses, bacteria and mold – You can heal through journeys to these beings and you can heal John, Diamond and other Dis-Eases that stress people. Homeopathic Remedies with the Vibrations of the various intelligences.

What is the purpose of our 2-D work?

Ultimately, the Purpose is for the People of the Earth to heal themselves by expanding their consciousness. Work with Your Family first, Blood Family. Infuse the Skulls that Cathy wants. Then your Spirit Family that is open. Marlene is a green go ahead. Eventually you will share the information, once honed, with Juanita and others including some from the Mending Medicine Group. For you will be the Survivors of the Earth's Shift because of your awareness and faith that all things are possible.

How is this related to the 13 Original Crystal Skulls?

The Crystal Skulls have Healing and Transformative Wisdom to share. It is important that you journey to them as well as ask questions thru the Akashic Records. Use your Akashic Prayer for Opening the Records to access information when not journeying. We will give you questions and use the 13 Moon Cycles for me specifically.

What does "Keepers of the Mary's" mean?

You hold Mary's healing energy by bringing forth these Prophesies and teaching about the Essential Oils. You are the light in darkness. You both have lines in the palms of making a giant M.

Are you a Mary? Do you have an M in the palms of your hand?

The left hand shows how you came in and the right shows what you have developed with your life experiences.

The explanation below was found a year after the original draft that was still a work in progress. It is humbling and profound and very relevant to telling the stories of Original 13 Crystal Skulls and their guardians and caregivers, who are "Mary's."

According to Clarrisa Pinkola Estes, PhD, in her book "*Untie the Strong Woman*" on page 242 she describes "The Marys":

"The Marys" are what we old believers call souls, both men and women, who have been sorely wounded, yet carry such depth of sight and generosity rather than bitterness of heart, that make you want to weep just to be near them again – or for the very first time...

The Marys everywhere in the world are the ones who endure despite, and in a way because of, all attacks, and all indecencies, against them. The Marys are the ones who were made to carry the World Heart in a basket woven strong from one's own courage bones, from spiritual brawn, from scar tissue, from the coiled hairs of one's own head. Beautiful.

Creator knew the pulse of the world would be safe with those who had suffered and yet preserved. Creator knew they would pass forward "that which cannot be allowed to perish from the face of the earth," hand to hand, heart to heart, generation to generation – hiding the Great Heart next to their own hearts during the night treks from village to village, no matter what crosswinds.

And most especially, The Marys would pass the Heart of the World soul to soul through stories that tell not just what is treasure, but that tell exactly how to hold to the strong center of the Mother no matter what."

As "Mary's" you are the reason and purpose for being given this assignment. You are to tell the stories of each individual skull of the Original 13 Crystal Skulls, the original Grandmothers.

How are Marlene and Marilee to work together?

You and Marlene are part of the original "Indigos" born in the late 1940's and 1950's – The "hippies" who came to transform, as agents of change. In September of 2012, James Twyman coined your group as the "Golden Indigos." Those people who quietly work continually with "dogged hope" as Barack Obama called it in his 2012 acceptance speech. You have always been connected energetically and each of you brings light to your area in your unique way.

Sometimes each of you will work together and sometimes you will work with others as your mission develops based on your choices. Sometimes you will work alone.

What are Marlene and Marilee to bring forth as part of our path, our life's work?

Marilee and Marlene are to work in the Akashic Records to bring forth Prayers and a new healing modality that works with the Telluric Realm. Providing Transformative Energy and Transformation – It is the next step. You and Marlene are Soul Sisters with similar work that is melded into a new way of Healing. It is a part of Your Life's Work, so is art, painting and fun. You both can write and writing is a gift you need to give – you need to Record in writing your adventures and healing.

What are we to do on January 31, 2011 to start the process of working with the 13 original crystal skulls and the Telluric Realm?

The Crystal Skulls are of the Telluric Realm. Work with 2 skulls per session on 4/25 work with the 13th Skull and journey to the Telluric ending on 6/25 for this part of the process. You will start your books after the Summer Solstice. You will write separate books in the same room.

(It turns out we could only work with one Skull per day, sometimes it was one Skull per week.
Marilee wrote her book over 26 months before the e-book was finished on March 31, 2013).

What roles do Marlene and I have together through past, present and future life times?

You have worked together in many dimensions and are of the same "POD" as part of the same Soul Group. You both as you know are part of "The Mary" Linage. Some call you Sophia – You are Healers of Group Energy. And, if you choose, all of your future work is in the higher realms with The Masters Teachers and Loved Ones. It was pre-ordained that this is your last Earth walk. Yet, you have much to do on the Earth plane. You will work with many people together in Ceremony and Ritual that Heals Miraculously. You will also assist many Transitions across the Veil – carrying people home – This is a gift. You and Marlene are balanced because each your twin flames are on the Earth. Marlene's twin flame is her twin sister Darlene and yours is your husband. You will teach the Way of Love; Accepting and Loving all who cross your paths.

SOURCES:

The Source of Information in our conversations is direct revelation from the Akashic Records and Shamanic Journeys to the Skulls themselves.
Dear Reader, you are asking:

"What are the Akashic Records?"
"What is a Shamanic Journey?"
"What is Quantum Healing?"

The Akashic Records and Shamanic Journeys are the perfect combination of the Divine Feminine and Masculine. It is the dancing of the yin and yang within us – activating the Quantum possibilities from Creator.

Receiving from the Akashic Record Information is Feminine because we open to receive the guidance and information from the Record Keepers.
Shamanic Journeys are Masculine. Our Souls travel out of our bodies seeking information, healing, guidance, wisdom to the beat of a frame drum to find the answers to our questions.

It is the rhythm of our heart beat which aligns us with the vibration of the Earth's Resonance Frequency called the Schumann Wave which is the same vibration as the human Alpha Brain Wave, also called the Shaman's Wave.

The Schumann Wave Frequency has increased as the Earth increased her vibration. The Schumann Wave has gone from 7.38Hrz to 7.83Hrz. To stay healthy and in alignment we must, each of us, raise our vibrations and frequencies.

The Alpha Brain Wave is called The Shaman's Wave for by entering the Alpha Brain Wave Frequency we are in alignment with Gaia. Gaia and the Schumann Wave are one and the same. Shamans enter a Shamanic State of Consciousness enabling them to travel into the multiple levels of the Inner Earth. They can enter Non-Ordinary Reality of the Earth to converse with the plants and animals and all living creatures. Lastly they can travel into the Universe and beyond. This is how the Mayans tracked Time.

PREPARATION:

Each Session starts with Meditation, Music and Incense to clear and ground us in preparation for our work.

When we open our Records we "Open To Receive" the Answers to our Questions and to any of the information that is given to us.

AKASHIC RECORDS:

On May 4, 2011 a New Definition came after I had a conversation earlier in the year with Linda Howe. I had explained that everything and everyone has their unique Vibration and Frequency. In April of 2002 I began to teach my clients to receive their own prayer aligned with their unique vibration. 2002 was also the year when Linda Howe presented her work and founded The Center for Akashic Studies. Linda Howe was my teacher for nine years from January of 1991 to January of 2000. The following is her definition:

"The Akashic Record is a Vibrational Record of every person's Soul and its journey. This Vibrational Record exists everywhere in its wholeness, and is completely available in all places. The Record contains all past, present, and future possibilities. It is an experiential body of knowledge and compassion."

10

The Akashic Records are known in the Bible as the Book of Life or Book of Remembrance. Every Being (be it human, animal, tree, rock, places or businesses and Each of the 13 Crystal Skulls) has a Spirit, Soul and an Akashic Record.

"AKASHA" is a Sanskrit word meaning Primordial Substance – That from which All Creation comes. The Akasha is also the Primordial Substance/Source of ALL KNOWLEDGE infused with Divine Love. Divine Love is the Vibration of Sound, Light and Color.

When accessing the Akashic Records, we can actually pull in higher vibrations. We start to raise our own vibration by using the Prayer and Centering ourselves. We set our Intention by writing down our questions. Because we are requesting specific information and guidance from the primordial Source of Creation and the Records of Light, we receive information from BEYOND our Energy Field - NOT from it. Yet the Akasha is everywhere at all times.

The Akasha itself has many layers also aligning with the charkas. In the Universe we actually have a minimum of thirteen Chakras or Energy Centers. The Earth has her own set of Records that are held by whales as Record Keepers and some say the Ica Stones. We each have an additional charka approximately a foot into the Earth and another chakra approximately 12 to 18 inches above our heads.

Reading the Akashic Records is receiving the Light infused with knowledge, wisdom and guidance from the Heart Center of Our Known Universe.

SHAMANISM:

Shamans and Indigenous storytellers hold the Records of the Earth and beyond in their oral traditions. Yet we too hold the legends of the Earth in our bones. The stones and bones hold the knowledge of all things. Our bodies are of the Earth minerals which hold information. So the deeper we go into ourselves the farther out into the Universe we can go to receive information. Shamans access information by traveling to the beat of a frame drum. They travel on the Sound Wave to access Non-Ordinary Reality (other worlds) where we can talk to the plants, animals, microbes and viruses.

We go deep to the beat of the drum to seek answers for ourselves, our families, our friends and our communities. When we Journey, we follow the ancient traditions of all the indigenous people of the Earth as we travel between the Worlds.

The original drummers were women from the inception of the drums in between 40, 000 and 25,000 BCE. The Women used single-headed drums for ceremonies for their family and Community.

The single-headed drum or frame drum is used around the globe to reach altered states of consciousness; to access the Beings of the Earth and the Universe who are waiting to guide us and help us. We must ask before we can receive the guidance and help they provide. That is their purpose, to help us live in alignment with the Earth and Universe. The Q'ero People make no distinction between Pachamama the Earth and Pachamama the Universe.

Indigenous Cultures and in Core Shamanism, as brought forth by Michael Harner, *KNOW* there are three Worlds:

LOWER WORLD – The Lower World is the Home of Stones, Crystals of all kinds, Plants, Animals, Elementals, Microbes, Health and Healing Guides. Answers to questions and conversations with these Beings are here unless taken elsewhere by our helpers.

MIDDLE WORLD - The Middle World is where we live. By journeying to Non-Ordinary reality here, we see, hear, know and feel information that we normally do not access or experience in our day to day lives. Here we can talk to our pets and trees.

UPPER WORLD – The Upper World is where we go to visit with our Guides and Helpers in Humanoid Form. This is where we go for guidance, solutions and related information. We travel through mists and visit crystal cities to find our teacher, guide, helper in the Upper World.

The Lower World is where we can be taken to get an answer or be shown how something works even though we went to the Upper World, or we may go to the Middle World or stay in the Upper World. The reverse is also true. We are taken to that place where the best answers to our questions are.

The Drum represents the womb (feminine receiver) and combined with the masculine beater stick (doing specific rhythms), creates anew by allowing us to find the answers to our questions. When we set our Intention with our questions, powerful allies show up with the answers.

Crystal Skulls are Allies with vast amounts of information to share with those they call. They are like Power Animals and more for they have knowledge from the great beyond of the multi-verses.

QUANTUM HEALING:

Quantum Healing is found in both the Akashic Records and Shamanic Journeys discussed briefly above and much more.

- It is Prayer and Meditation, which is how we start each session, setting our Intention.
- It is a Walk in the woods communing with Nature.
- It is alone time when you listen to the small quiet voice. When we transcribe our notes and receive more information.
- It is Native American Ceremony; Drum Circles; Vision Quests; Purification Lodges.

There is classical physics or Newtonian Physics dealing with phenomena involving dimensions larger than an atom.

Then there is quantum physics, which has to do with anything smaller than an atom, things too small to experience with any of our five senses. These include electrons, neutrons, protons, quarks, neutrinos, mesons and other subatomic particles. These can all be accessed with Shamanic Journeys.

With Quantum Physics the experimenter is always a part of the experiment and the observer's intention is a part of the whole – there is no separation.

We operate in a Quantum World where Light manifests as a wave described by frequencies, amplitude, and phase (numbers) or as a stream of particles with properties of discrete quanta described by size and other material quantities. These quantum particles are called photons.

The speed of Quantum Biofeedback Stress Reducing devise is one/one hundredth of a second. The entire human body can be scanned over 110 channels and over 20,000 plus frequencies in three minutes.

The information produced in the three minute scan shows where the body is stressed and what it needs to balance and which stressors are ready to be reduced. This "Quantum Phenomena" is only possible because of piezoelectric quartz crystal. This is the same material used in the computer circuitry and the Intelligence of the quantum Biofeedback machine called a SCIO, which means "to know". Amber is also piezoelectric.

It is Quantum Phenomena. The Mitchell – Hedges Crystal Skull of Love and the Original 13 Crystal Skulls are made of piezoelectric quartz crystal, the same material used in computer circuitry. You see the link between the Crystal Skulls and Knowledge.

The Skulls as well as computer circuitry are alive with knowledge, wisdom and information. The Skulls are accessed using my Akashic Records Prayers and direct communication via Shamanic Journeys traveling the sound waves to the Skulls for direct revelation.

These are the two methods that I use to Access the information that we were requested to bring forth by the Lords of Light of the Akashic Records. For a deeper explanation refer to the diagram in Resources.

We ask the same questions getting different, but related information based on what we resonate with. First we open Our Own Records with our Individual Prayers for an hour or two depending on our preparation time. We break for lunch or a snack. We return to our Sacred Space to journey to the Skulls with questions given. We tried to keep the questions uniform for each Skull.

Please enjoy the Conversation that came from our Research (Resources and a Bibliography at the end) and our work with the Akashic Records and our Shamanic Journeys.

For me personally, this has been an extra-ordinary experience of Healing and Transformation as I continually clear the spiritual and emotional blockages to make this book possible. All of my continual Healing since January of 2011 has been Spiritual with the assistance of Shamanic Healing, Young Living Essential Oils and miraculous Quantum Healing with Prayer and Meditation facilitated by magnificent Shamans and Healers.

Writing and sharing this information with you is very experiential for me as I walk with my feet in two Worlds; two Paradigms learning so that I can share more and more with the World and You Dear Reader...

The next portion is the condensed story of my life.

HOW I GOT HERE:

Much of this is from my chapter in the anthology *"Pebbles In The Pond— Transforming the World One Person at a Time."* It is my story of transformation and conscious expansion of my awareness so that I can share my knowledge and experiences with you, my traveling companion, in this great adventure called Life. Here is my story.

Death and Beyond – Heaven on Earth

According to Merlin, "A wizard is someone who lives their life backwards." I am a wizard. I died at 26, became an entrepreneur at 36, discovered spirituality and Shamanism at 46, married at 56, and became a published author at 66.

On December 12, 1972, I was working for the Australian Consulate in Chicago. I was in my office coughing when co-workers said I really needed to go to the hospital. So, off I went to the emergency room.

In the ER, I was told my right lung had collapsed from a body full of blood clots. I was NOT going anywhere except to a hospital room, then to the nuclear lab. I was sitting on the side of the bed smoking a cigarette when they brought oxygen for me, totally unaware of how "sick" I was.

No one honestly believed my survival was possible. The doctor said, "You will die. All we can do is to give you oxygen and blood thinners every four hours to dissolve the blood clots. But, if you survive, you can never have children, need to lose 50 pounds, and quit smoking." I told him no one was knocking at my door.

The next thing I knew, I was in the upper corner of my room looking down at my body lying in bed. Everything was grey: my body, the sheets, walls and floor. Then there was THE LIGHT.

The air was different; it shimmered and sparkled, full of crystal particles. It was soft, like mother of pearl, shimmering very pale colors of pink, lavender, turquoise, yellow gold and silver white, nothing I have ever experienced on Earth. I can go there any time as if it just happened.

Lush green rolling hills climbed gently towards a low line of purple mountains. Behind the mountains was the most extraordinarily bright, luminous Light of gold and white, very different from the air. It was "The Other Side." I heard an almost inaudible singing and felt soothed, caressed, and nurtured.

Faces with no bodies greet me. I know them – my great-grandparents and my Granddaddy. "The Other Side" feels very safe and loving. For the first time I can remember, I have no physical, mental, emotional, or spiritual pain. There is just the most incredible sense of peace, unconditional love, and compassion for myself, everyone, and everything.

Feeling safe allowed me to hear my family say, "The choice to stay and never feel pain again is yours."

For up to this moment, my life had been filled with fear and pain from orthopedic surgeries, continual psychic attacks, plus the emotional and benign neglect of my mother. I had taken on her fears, trying to make everything "okay" to make her like me.

Then there was my brother's alcoholic abuse which escalated upon his return from two tours in Viet Nam. My mother never acknowledged his addiction. During this same time, at 23, I was raped at gunpoint after moving to Chicago's Near North. I came home only to be sent to my room. Mom never once discussed the incident. I had a figure like Sophia Loren, yet Mom continually gave me mixed messages saying that I was fat, ugly, yet extremely intelligent. It wasn't fun being me.

As I stared at this incredible bright loving Light, my life flashed before me. For the first time, I knew "God" existed, and is loving, kind, and compassionate; a huge revelation for an agnostic.

In an instant there was a knowing. I remember saying to my Grandparents, "I have to go back. There is something that I have to do." No specifics, just that I was to go back. I woke up in the most excruciating pain, like I was being stabbed in the back on my right side. For the fifth time in 26 years I was hospitalized.

What I remember the most from my Death experience was this incredible gift of LOVE, actually experiencing it for the first time. It has been a long continual journey of transformation and remembering who I really am in each decade from the beginning to now.

Grace and faith came to me with the shifting from linear to circular thinking, trusting my knowing. Learning that as a small child full of light, I did know the Truth. I remember saying to my friends, "My heart is so full of love, and I don't know what to do with it."

"Your vision will become clear only when you can look into your own heart. Who looks outside, dreams; who looks inside, awakens." – Carl Jung

Our vision is a reality – Heaven on Earth. We live on 21 acres of woodland called Sage Spirit Terra, meaning "Healing Spirit Land." It is a long way from Chicago, and many years in the making, for first it was a vision that started long ago in the dreamtime.

Yet in 1963, everything had changed. I'd won every award available in my first year of Junior Achievement going to the National Convention. Then my Dad told me they were moving to Chicago and left me behind in Indiana to finish high school. Everyone moved in August. In September my Granddaddy died, leaving me with my grieving Grandmother.

In 1965, I needed my father's written permission to attend Purdue University's Krannert School of Business. Paying for my own education, I graduated in 1969, one of five women.

After healing from the blood clots and receiving emotional counseling, one day in 1974, I quit my job and booked a flight to Italy. Thanks to a pickpocket in Milan, I lived creatively on $400.00 and my rail pass for six weeks. I started to awaken.

Upon returning, friends put me to work renting subsidized housing in a Chicago ghetto, which led to a successful career in real estate nationwide. Dale Carnegie classes in 1976 helped me with self-esteem, but I still did not know or love myself.

In 1982, I met Sonia Choquette who gave me a reading and said, "Marilee, you need to make the inside as beautiful as the outside." What I have since learned is transformational healing comes from the inside out, from above down on the whisperings of Spirit.

In 1982, I attended a Landmark/est. weekend. I founded my first business marketing and managing high-rise buildings in Chicago. In 1988, I opened "Gold Coast Cleaning & Contracting." This gave me weekends and evenings off to study in my sacred secret garden. After fourteen years, I gave the business to my employees.

Rumi said, "Your task is not to seek for love, but merely to seek and find all the barriers within yourself that you have built against it."

From the 1991 to now my healing and growth has been exponential. Linda Howe taught me the Akashic Records. Michael Harner and Sandra Ingerman are my Shamanic teachers for journeying, extraction, divination, Soul Retrieval, and carrying Souls home. Michael Soto is Reiki Master to Anthony Pizzoferrato, my Reiki Master. Each provided spiritual awakening with direct revelation, insights, experiential, and transformational healings and many initiations.

Indigenous Teachers started coming in 2000. Ipupiara and Cleicha came to my "Healing Waters" event on the crystalline sands of Lake Michigan in 2001 and 2002, which we continued with our store, Earth Partners, a spiritual store where we met the Mitchell-Hedges crystal skull. I learned quantum healing with Young Living Essential Oils, with extensive training I became Internationally Certified in Quantum Biofeedback. In 2005, I was initiated as a Purification Lodge Keeper and Pipe Carrier. Each modality is quantum healing because it is from Source/God, Creator.

In 2007, using everything I know plus forgiveness of myself, I transmuted the cancer in my liver, right lung, and breast as my deceased sister stood guard. When the forgiveness was complete, she left, covering me with a blanket of light. I was then awarded a Sundance Buffalo Skull in May and hosted the World Drum in July at Sage Spirit Terra.

During these years I cried buckets of tears as I experienced many setbacks, deaths, and bankruptcy. With continual meditation, prayer, forgiveness, and ceremony, my consciousness expanded to include, to accept, and to embrace, both the light and the darkness, including those souls that lower their light to teach.

In dying, the Shaman is shown the Oneness of the web of life. I experienced "The Light" as the light of individual souls, like the individual leaves on black tree branches of the One Tree. By definition, I am "Wounded Healer/Shaman" learning to heal myself to help others.

In 2011, I was given a new assignment. "Write about the original 13 crystal skulls." To write, once a month, for six months, I needed soul retrievals to remove the fear, doubt, and pain, and receive Love, confidence, and trust.

Shifting into my heart, I continually heal my barriers to love raising my vibration and consciousness, thus allowing space for you to make the paradigm shift to be kinder and more loving. I came back to love you as your spiritual guide, healer, and teacher.

What will you do?

After "Pebbles in the Pond" launched on May 20, 2012; as my journey continued. By not listening to my own words, I lost my ability to market anything. I was "taken out" To BE. I gained more wisdom and knowledge in an almost exponential way and I was able to submit a manuscript to a Hay House writing contest. I didn't win but learned much.

As I was "Being" all kinds of invitations came to me. All accepted and the Third Annual Hot Springs Crystal and Crystal Skull Conference is in October of 2013 and I am a presenter and participating in the opening ceremony which came to several of us in bits and pieces during a New Moon Drum Circle.

As of March 2013, I am very excited to share with you that I am now the caretaker of five Skulls. Never in my wildest dreams did I think I would be writing about crystal skulls let alone caring for them. As of August 3, 2013, I became the proud guardian of another 6 Skulls giving me 13 Crystal Skulls. As I write, two remain quiet as to their names. I am waiting patiently.

My first Skull, Rose (rose quartz) who has been with me for 11 years since I bought it in 2002 for our store, Earth Partners (full of crystals and semi-precious stones). My niece Cathy was the only person interested in it, but something inside told me to keep it. It is now named Rose and there is a tiny blue Sodalite Skull named Blue Rose that came as a gift in the fall of 2011; Star Child arrived as a gift on 12.12.12 on the 40th Anniversary of my NDE; Mona Marie, a small striped Fluorite skull, was given to me on Halloween of 2012 when we hosted the World Drum and Cydonia, who arrived in August of 2012(the only one who called and I consciously bought until a week ago). The names of the first two skulls only came after Cydonia arrived. Three of the Skulls represent the Triple Goddess – The three phases of the Divine feminine. In June of 2013, Yin, a Hematite Skull and Yang, a quartz Crystal Skull came together.

The next set of six Skulls is a large blue Sodalite Skulls, a Sardonyx Skull both unnamed as I write. A Jade Skull wants to be called Jade. An Orange Carnelian just told me her name is Creativity. A deep purple Fluorite that

19

looks like amethyst is Gratitude. The Moss Agate skull with hollows in the back like Ocean Jasper told me her name is See Mother.

This quote has been waiting for See Mother, I think. *Proverbs 1.8 says "Do Not Ignore the Teachings of Your Mother."*

In 1992, I learned that my Mother and Your Mother are the same - the Earth, herself. Her teachings represent the Divine Mother of all Indigenous Teachings and of the Shekinah of the Kabbalah and the Bible.

Our culture is patriarchal in its design and function, leaving little or no room for the Sacred Feminine. It is time for Patriarchy to step aside making room for and bringing forth the Divine Feminine in full and equal partnership with the Divine Masculine culturally and within each individual and being – within and without.

This book "Ancient Wisdom for NOW" brings through this knowledge via Ancient 13 Crystal Skulls.

In my mind, the 13 Crystal Skulls are the Original Grandmothers' teaching balance with generosity, trust, forgiveness, compassion, kindness, loving with respect and gratitude and patience, especially for the Elders and Children, our teachers.

The 13 Grandmother Skulls show us how to create and experience our own divinity as we create our Sacred Spaces, gathering in Circles to "Remember"; to drum, to share, to receive direct revelation from our shamanic journeys for our highest and best good.

The conversation is with these Original 13 Crystal Skulls about the Earth, the Mayan Medicine Wheel, Ceremony, Ritual, The Akashic Records, Shamanic Journeys, Quantum Healing and much more.

The healing brought forth will be presented in Book III of the Trilogy *"Ancient Wisdom for NOW! - Natural Healing with Shamanism including Creator's Gift – Therapeutic Grade Essential Oils."*

Before we talk to the 13 Crystal Skulls sharing what they have to say along with what five well known Crystal Skull Guardians have to say about their experiences, let us explore the Legends of the Crystal Skulls.

Are the Legends Truth?

You decide what feels right for you and resonates with your Soul.

Here they are:

LEGENDS OF THE CRYSTALS:

Many believe that there is a strong connection between the crystals skulls, the Mayans and the Mayan Calendar ending December 21, 2012. In recent years, the Mayans have spearheaded a grand reunion of North America's indigenous chiefs in an effort to unite forces, and gather the 13 Crystal Skulls.

- Where are the Skulls?
- Where did they come from?
- What is their purpose?

ATLANTIS LEGEND:

Of the 13 Ancient Skulls that are clear quartz crystal the where about of only three of the ancient singing Skulls are known. Bill Homann is one such guardian. He claims that his Skull, the M-H Skull of Love is from Atlantis. The other ten are buried in the Earth and scattered in the five directions including the Ethers.

This corresponds with information received from Dolores Cannon's book *"The Three Waves of Volunteers and THE NEW EARTH"*. Chapter 31 is called THE KEEPERS OF THE GRID. This story is of a woman who remembers her time in Atlantis and her fascination with crystals. She had a store that sold crystals this life time as did my husband and I.

What she related so resonated in my Soul. Since I received my Quantum Biofeedback Machine (QXCI/SCIO) in June of 2003, I have seen myself in a crystal room with three other practitioners trying to raise the vibrations of people. The room looks like giant sheets of crystal that looks like striated ice.

It is my belief that many of us came back to help the Earth so the destruction of Atlantis doesn't happen again. We are headed in that direction with the C.E.R.N. Reactor in Switzerland. This Reactor works with Dark Matter which collapses things. During the time of Atlantis the Dark Matter work was so powerful that it threaten to collapse the Earth Grid and beyond with

21

Universal ramifications...It was decided that before the destruction occurred that all of the technology would be put in Crystals and Crystal skulls. The Crystal skulls are vast Libraries of information. They were sent out to the 4 corners of the Earth and beyond for the preservation of the knowledge, wisdom, information and technology. Then only Atlantis was collapsed intentionally from the outside.

Remember Crystal, and Crystal Skulls expand the Light, Wisdom and Information and dark matter collapses in on itself destroying what the Light and expansion with Love. Crystals expands Light and Love. Light and Sound are the source of all vibration and frequencies in our ever expanding Universe and in the Multiverses.

HIMALYAN MOUNTAINS (TIBET?):

My friend Deane Gemmell is The Saga-Oracle. She created our crystal Skull diagrams and she wrote *"Jeshua's Song"* stories that fascinates and teaches far beyond the Crucifixion. It is the story of a very heretical pagan Jeshua (Jesus) his life including his wife, Mary Magdelene and their four children and it includes a "Legend".

The legend in Chapter Thirty-Two *"The Healing Skull of Mu "*according to this story, Jesus was removed from the cave and taken to the high mountains of his youth where he was again greeted by his Teacher and his Guardian, each a Master. They cleaned him and kept his body alive while he bi-located to talk with his family and closest followers. This is what we call Easter Sunday. Then he returned to cave in what we call the Himalayan Mountains.

There in seclusion with the Healers and Masters with the Skull of Mu beside his head, the healing began. All seven bodies were receiving the healing energy of this Skull. The seven bodies are the Soul, Spiritual, Emotional, Mental, Etheric, Astral and Physical all in one Being, all having their own function, purpose and properties with the physicality of the person. Each individual has these seven bodies.

The beauty and frequencies of this Skull of Mu was enough to raise the vibrations of all present, allowing for internal and external healing. It is said that this is an actual skull crystallized from the head-bones of a great master from the Land of Mu with a succession of guardians, care-takers and keepers – Each person learns something different from the Skull to put into service. In this story the Monks were scooping Light from the Skull of Mu and putting it in the dark spots of Jeshua's body aura where there were blockages to full recovery.

The Skull of Mu is described as Sky-Blue Crystal. When Deanne sat with the Mitchell-Hedges Skull of Love, she felt that they might be the same Skull although its current guardian says it from Atlantis. When you read Linda (Allayah) Frisch's story – you will find that some of the ancient Mongolian and Himalayan Skulls were covered in tree resin to dim their light so they were safe until needed.

In France there is a black Crystal Skull that is said to be the head of Mary Magdelene that crystallized representing the Black Madonna. It is on display in a church as seen by a friend and Medicine Woman of the Lakota Sioux.

NORTH and SOUTH AMERICAN LEGENDS:

There are many Native American legends that have been handed down for thousands of years, as Lia Scallon writes on her website. From the Mayan and Aztec versions of Central America to the Pueblo and Navajo in the South Western United States, the Lakota of the Plains and also including the Cherokee and Seneca Nation variations from the Eastern United States. In essence the basic legend is the same.

It states that there are 13 Ancient Crystal Skulls. These are the size of real human skulls and have movable jaws enabling them to speak and sing. It is said the 13 Crystal Skulls have encoded within them the origin, purpose and destiny of mankind as well as the answers to all the greatest mysteries of life in the universe.

(It is my personal belief that the13 Ancient Crystal Skulls hold information from the Multi-verse that far exceeds the Akashic Records of this Universe and this planet in particular. With Shamanic Journeys we have access to this wisdom.)

The legend claims that, one day, all 13 Crystal Skulls will be discovered and brought together and their collective wisdom will be revealed. However, the human race must first be sufficiently evolved, both morally and spiritually so as not to abuse the knowledge.

The Twisted Hairs Society includes members of over 400 different indigenous nations that represent all of North, South and Central America. They tell a more detailed version.

"Long ago North, South and Central America, along with the continents that are now called New Zealand and Australia, were all one land mass, all one continent known to our people as 'Turtle Island'.

The elders of the Twisted Hairs said that in the very beginning there were 12 worlds with human life. The cosmic elders met on a planet called Osiriaconwiya. They met to discuss the plight of the 'planet of the children' where we are today. It is called that because it is the least evolved of all the planets with human life. So we are one of a family of 12 planets.

Each of the other planets took the sum total of all their knowledge and encoded it in what can best be described, in modern terms, as a holographic image computer called a crystal skull. These are absolutely flawless, perfect Crystal Skulls. These skulls have moving jaws just like our skulls so they were referred to as 'the singing skulls' and the entire configuration was known as 'the Ark of Osiriaconwiya'. Each Crystal Skull represents a different planet's knowledge. They helped the people of Earth build four great civilizations of Lemuria, Mu, Mieyhun and Atlantis.

To help with the teachings, other Crystal Skulls were created here on Earth and although life-size, their jaws do not move and they are known as 'the talking skulls'.

The Crystal Skulls were kept inside a pyramid in a formation of tremendous power known as the Ark. The Ark was comprised of the 12 Crystal Skulls from each of the sacred planets kept in a circle with a 13th skull, being the largest; placed in the center. The 13th skull represents the collective consciousness of all the worlds. This ark connects the knowledge of all the sacred planets.

As the Spanish were about to seize the Crystal Skulls, Jaguar Priests and Eagle Warriors took the skulls and fled with them. And so the 13 Crystal Skulls were separated for the first time in their history. It is said they will be brought together again when we learn to share with one another, care for one another, teach one another, heal one another and live in peace and harmony with Grandmother Earth.

The above legend is posted on the internet by Lia Scallon at http://www.soundsofsirius.com/crystalskulls.html

MAYAN LEGEND:

According to Mayan Priest/Shaman, Don Alejandro Cirilo Oxlaj Peres: "... The prophecy says now is the time of the awakening. This is your job now, to awaken. The Vale of the Nine Hells is past and the Time of Warning has now arrived. It is time to prepare for the Age of the Thirteen Heavens. The time of 12 Baktun and 13 Ahau is fast approaching, and they shall be here among you to defend Mother Earth.

The prophecy says, 'Let the dawn come. Let all the people and all the creatures have peace, let all things live happily', for the love must not only be between humans, but between all living things. They said, 'We are the children of the sun, we are the children of time and we are the travelers in space. May all the songs awaken; May all the dancers awaken. May all the people and all things live in peace for you are the valleys, you are the mountains, you are the trees, you are the very air you breathe'. Now is the time of return of the grandmothers and grandfathers. Now is the time of the return of the Elders. Now is the time of the return of the Wise Ones. And the Wise Ones are all of you. Now is the time to go out into the world and spread the light. The sacred flame has been kept for this purpose and now the time approaches when you will be required to love all things, to love a world that has gone crazy, to rebalance the heavens and the Earth. For the Time of Warning has come to pass; the Warriors of the Rainbow are now being born. The Vale of Tears, the Nine Hells, is over and it is time to prepare for the 13 Heavens. The ancestors are returning, my brothers and sisters, and we do not have long. Now is the time that the prophecies will be fulfilled."

During November of 2011, 13 Crystal Skulls gathered at Cahokia, Hopi Land, Sedona and Los Angeles.

MEXICAN LEGEND:

The Huichol Shamans of Northwest Mexico, who are extensively trained in the use of crystals, and walking in two worlds to bring forth healing with rituals and ceremonies.

Indigenous Shamans know that when clear quartz crystal becomes hot from a fire or from the energy of the shamans they become empowered. That empowerment is then transferred to the client/patient or to the village.

Among the Huichol people it is believed that a shaman's Soul may be reincarnated in the form of a quartz crystal. The crystal quartz then passes on the shaman's wisdom and knowledge.

Is there any relationship to clear quartz Skulls that Mayan priest's put on stones sitting on top of a fire until the skull glowed? Is this the transference of "power", Healing and knowledge?

AFRICAN LEGEND:

An African tribe, the Dogon, have always maintained that their ancestors came from Sirius which they said had a double star system. No one believed them until telescopes became powerful enough to confirm what they claimed to be true.

One of my important teachers Dr. Bernardo Piexoto, Anthropologist at the Smithsonian, is also known as Ipupiara a Master Healer Medicine Man from Brazil. His tribe call themselves "People of the Stars" as do many Native American Nations. It is a common belief among the various nations.

Others say we came from Earth. Both are correct. That is why DNA has two strands. Originally one strand contained our Earth memories and the other our celestial heritage memories. Scientists are now close to confirming this.

Possibly one of the reasons why the Crystal Skulls were made of silicon quartz is because silicon was introduced into our genetic structure by the sky gods. Within us is a part of the whole crystalline matrix that can link us to the rest of the universe. Indigenous people have always known the Earth, sun and all the other planets are linked by an enormous crystalline web-like structure. This web is made of sound, light and color just as the Original 13 Skulls are a part of this web and they have their own matrix with it.

These are some of the legends surrounding the Crystal Skulls. You choose the legend or that part of each legend that works for you in this moment.

Your perception, concepts and consciousness may just change.

Are You Ready? THE TIME IS NOW!

MORE LEGENDS:

Here are more Legends/Truths around the Original 13 Crystal Skulls.

The most famous of the Skulls – The Mitchell-Hedges Skull is pictured on our cover resting on the 90% quartz crystal sand of Lake Michigan in Northwest Indiana. (Picture provided by Bill Homann, owner and caretaker, who received the Skull in 2007 from Anna Mitchell – Hedges. Anna cared for this Skull until her 100th year, when she left the Earth plane.)

Anna gave the Skull to her husband, the new guardian on his birthday because she found it on her birthday in 1924. The last years of her life were spent in Northwest Indiana in the care of Bill Homann, the current caretaker and guardian of the Crystal Skull. They lived near Lake Michigan and the Indiana Dunes National Lake Shore where the sand is 90 percent Quartz Crystal, the "Singing Sands."

In Part II is an interview with Bill Homann. Prior to even thinking about writing this book, I had the privilege of meeting and being in the presence of the Mitchell-Hedges Skull on two different occasions. Although, the M-H Skull came to me often in my dreams, beginning in 2002.

Jamie Sams, of the Seneca Nation, wrote a book called "The Thirteen Original Clan Mothers." I bought it when I was in Santa Fe in 1993. Twenty years later it has been read and read and re-read.

In this book each Moon Cycle is represented by a Skull and Shield. Jamie Sams sums up the importance of the Original 13 Crystal Skulls beautifully, by writing:

"We are now entering the Time of the Quickening. That is why it is time to tell about the crystal skulls and their connection with our origins. Only after all the knowledge and wisdom of the crystal skulls has found its way into all the peoples' hearts will the Fifth World of Illumination truly begin.
The crystal skulls can provide us with an access point into these other dimensions, where we can begin to see our connections with all other things. The crystal skulls show us that we need to awaken to this knowledge, that we need to wake up to our connection with each other and with this Mother Earth that sustains us, and that we need to start to repair and celebrate these connections in our lives."

In 2002 after I had ordered a large variety of crystals and books for our new store, Earth Partners I found and read the Mysteries of the Crystal Skull. Then the Mitchell Hedges Skull often visited me in my dreams, healing me and telling me her stories of healing. Crystals have been a part of my life for over 22 years and I have lived on the crystal "Singing Sands" since we moved to Northwest Indiana in 1996.

Then in 2003 we added a Quantum Biofeedback Machine to our store offerings to provide stress reduction. It is claimed by some that the SCIO is Atlantean technology and that this area of Northwest Indiana on the Eastern shore of Lake Michigan were a part of Atlantis. There are people with karma reborn to this area that worked with the crystals, crystal skulls and the advanced crystal technologies of Atlantis that desecrated the Earth. We are here to heal that damage and the damage that is repeating itself in our culture of corporate greed.

The Prophecy of the Crystal Skulls has been around for hundreds of years and there are different versions depending on who is telling the story.

It is well known that the Mayan calendar ends abruptly at midnight on December 21, 2012. Several other cultures also predict that the world would end in 2012, or will it?

It Did NOT. The Sun may shift it Axis, but we are here NOW!!

The Prophecies are told to bring about change so that what is predicted never comes to be. They worked. *The Time is NOW!*

Other legends say this date marks the end of our struggle on Earth and can only be changed by bringing the 13 Crystal Skulls together. When they are brought together they will enlighten us as to how we can live in better harmony with each other and the Earth. It is a new beginning.

The Time is NOW!

This is the time of the Mended Medicine Wheel of our Milky Way when an equilateral cross of Light appears in the Sky on December 21, 2012. We must mend our personal Medicine Wheels and the Original 13 Crystal Skulls are our teachers and healers in this endeavor.

They certainly have assisted and pushed me and continue to do so beyond what is written in the chapter called "How I Got Here".

The Maya are the Time Keepers and the Keepers of Knowledge. This is what another Elder has to say about the Skulls and this time.

Patricio Dominguez - Pueblo Spiritual Advisor:

"The crystal skulls are complete depositories of knowledge and each skull contains a particular specialist area of information–like a living library (each skull is like one volume in a set of encyclopedias.) And the people who will in the future be able to 'read' the crystal skulls when they are all assembled together. Once they are assembled will we humans be able to extract all the knowledge ... Of course, the knowledge that is going to come from the skulls is quite unimaginable to our current minds. But that it is definitely going to come out at a certain time is already foregone. It has been prophesied. But whether we humans then use that knowledge for good or for our own destruction is really down to our preparations."

The Time Is NOW!

PART II

A CONVERSATION WITH THE ORIGINAL 13 CRYSTAL SKULLS AND FIVE CRYSTAL SKULL GUARDIANS

This section used to be two distinct parts. One was the Conversations with the Original 13 Crystal Skulls and one part was just the Crystal Skull Guardians sharing some of their experiences. We are honored to have these contributors in order of agreeing to participate: Gina O'Connor, Kristen Hilling, Bill Homann, Joshua Shapiro and Linda (Allayah) Frisch.

First, I want to thank and express my deep gratitude and appreciation to each person who gave their time, expertise and caring to contribute their personal experiences caretaking their Crystal Skulls. Their Generosity and Kindness and Patience with me and this book speak to the magnificence of their Souls. I'm sure they never thought they'd see a copy since three contributed in the Spring of 2011 and then one more in August/September of 2012 and the last contribution March 2013.

In getting to know the caretakers and guardians of crystal skulls, my world and my heart have expanded from the generous love that each one shares effortlessly. They in turn have introduced me to a community of people that are kind, patient filled with compassion and respect for all life on Earth, in the Universe and the Multiverse. This is a like-minded family of Soul friends.

As you read these interviews and articles you will see how all of these people have worked together supporting each other's work with the Crystal Skulls to get the message of cooperation, balance, harmony, Healing and Love into the mass consciousness of humanity.

The journey intensified my own Spiritual growth and healing as many caretakers can attest to. I never thought at age 65 I'd be starting accelerated career learning from these teaching crystal skulls, writing and speaking to my healing and my services, but here I am.

Now, I too am the caretaker of 13 Skulls as I write. I received the third Skull Cydonia in August of 2012. This Skull called to me via the internet and I bought it from my friend Gina. Then I was told to get Kirsten's Crystal Skull Cards and Book. They too arrived in August to help me finish this book. Each time I've needed to write to meet a deadline Skulls appear in my life to help and support me.

On August 13, 2012 Joshua Shapiro held an on-line 13 Crystal Skull Meditation for Peace. The Skulls came to me with a healing for my left (feminine) knee and directed me to contact Joshua so that he could contribute if he chose to.

Joshua has contributed an article. I realized that all that has happened in August was necessary before I was able to finish this book and submit it by the September 27, 2012 deadline. I had wanted to submit it on the Blue Moon of August 31. I submitted it on The Autumn Equinox per my guidance.

At this time I'd like to introduce these incredible people from around the World who care for and work with Crystal Skulls. They are listed in alphabetical order by their first name:

Gina O'Connor from the United States and Holland, who cares for Skulls, finds them homes and is the Director for International Spiritual Experience. She is helping to organize as well as speak at the Second Annual Crystal Skull Conference and will be participating in the Third Annual Crystal Skull Conference in Hot Springs, AR.

Joshua Shapiro and Katrina Head are the Crystal Skull Explorers, from near Seattle, Wash., USA. Joshua has been working with Crystal Skulls for 30 years and he is offering free e-book from Amazon.com as well as monthly meditations through facebook on the 13th day on the 13th hour once a month. He has worked with all of the other contributors.

Kirsten Hilling of Germany, Author, Creator Crystal Card Deck, International Speaker, Teacher, Spiritual Guide and caretaker a large Crystal Skull Family including the Smoky Quartz Skull called Kasper and others including White Buffalo Calf Woman.

Linda (Allayah) Frisch is from New Jersey, USA. Linda lives near Princeton University and has worked with the Ancient Skulls and Jade Disc since 2000. Her fascination came after a serious surgery on the back of her that resulted in a NDE. Her husband bought her a computer to communicate and recover from the damage done to her. She met Frank Loo and the rest is history. Her story is one of hope and courage. She uses her NDE re-wiring to help people with her psychic readings as guided by the Skulls.

William " Bill" Homann – Guardian and Caretaker of the Mitchell-Hedges Skull of Love who spreads the message of Love while working with John of God, creating two "Casas"—one in Sedona, Arizona and in Italy, triangulating the energy of Love between Italy, Arizona and Brazil.

Bill was so kind by offering his help and by giving us a few of the pictures of the M-H Skull of Love in this book.

As expressed at the beginning of this section, my Heart is filled with deep Appreciation and Gratitude to each of these contributors. It has been such fun meeting them, getting to know them and their missions. Each of them is truly of Service to Mankind.

The 30 year veteran is our first guardian to share his story. Here is Joshua; after Joshua will be Skull I, Skull 2 and Skull 3 followed by Linda (Allayah) Frisch then the next set of 3 Skulls 4,5,6 then Gina O'Connor followed by the 3 Skulls 7,8, 9 and then Kristen Hilling followed by Skulls 10,11, 12 and 13 then Bill Homann's interview.

A Crystal Skull Explorer - 30 Years of Adventures and Travels
By: R. Joshua Shapiro

Like most people I have met over the years, I didn't have a plan that I would be involved with Crystal Skulls for such a long time or even a visible sign that something would come up. But due to all the wonderful people I have met along the way and the amazing Crystal Skulls themselves, I would not trade this life for anything else.

As a typical Aries man, I have a love for adventure, new journeys, variety and challenge and this is exactly what happens when you bring the crystal skulls into your life. Through the interest to study the Crystal Skulls I met my beloved Katrina, who has agreed to join me on this journey of life and to become the other part of the Crystal Skull Explorers. This is the best way we can describe ourselves being linked to this tremendous work to provide the best information and insights we can about these amazing artifacts.

How it all started for me was a visit to a metaphysical bookstore in San Jose, California, one sunny day in April of 1983. The Ram Metaphysical Bookstore was owned by my good friend Franciose Beaudoin. I was just going to visit with Francoise and see if she needed more copies of my first book, "Journeys of an Aquarian Age Networker" (published in 1982). Then all of a sudden, during our conversation, she pulled out a special photograph to share and little did I know this photograph would forever change my life. The picture activated my inner knowing and memory of a part of the spiritual work I was born to do to help our world and all the living creatures living upon and within the "Mother Earth."

So what was this photograph you ask?

Well, it was a picture of a Crystal Skull, of course. Francoise and her friend Stephen had this Crystal Skull in their possession for a short time and were even able to keep this skull in their homes. The Crystal Skull in the photograph was made out of amethyst quartz. It apparently was discovered in Mexico, as I understood it, in a cache with other Mayan artifacts probably near some ancient Mesoamerican ruins, although the true history might never be known.

Apparently a Mayan Priest in Mexico had come into contact with this Crystal Skull and had brought it to San Jose, California. Stephen was invited to view the skull, as he is a spiritual archaeologist. Through Stephen, Francoise had her opportunity to meet this Crystal Skull during 1983 when it was simply called the "Amethyst Crystal Skull." The few people who met this crystal skull at that time felt it was possibly a very old activated Skull.

Anyway to discuss my first contact with a crystal skull, let me share my experiences in the order in which they happened.

First I saw the photograph of this Amethyst Crystal Skull at Francoise bookstore. As I viewed the photo I felt a strong shaking taking place on the inside of my body like an inner earthquake. About a half an hour later, there was a real earthquake in Coalinga, California, about 150 miles or so south of San Jose. The table the picture of the Amethyst Crystal Skull was sitting on was vibrating fiercely. Then somehow an insight came to me as I gazed at this photo that the Crystal Skulls collectively were vital for the future of humanity and there seemed to be an invitation that I was being given indirectly to help in this process. But first I hoped I could see this Amethyst Crystal Skull in person.

In May of 1983 the arrangements were made. The Amethyst Crystal Skull was stored in a vault at an art gallery and I was invited to attend a showing of this crystal skull at this location. During this showing I was allowed to touch the Crystal Skull. I initially touched the top part of the skull with my right hand. As I did so, I felt a strong energy move from hand, up into my arm and stop at my right shoulder. After this, in my mind's eye I could see this Amethyst Skull floating behind me over my right shoulder. So the Amethyst Skull most definitely served as a catalyst to help me began my journey with the crystal skulls.

Until I traveled to Oakland, California, in 1985, all I had was a few photos of this crystal skull to share with other people. At an open meeting I attended in this area, I did a talk about UFOs showing a video of purportedly real live UFOs that appeared in Switzerland. During my presentation, a woman raised her hand and discussed something with me about the Crystal Skulls. The woman turned out to be Sandra Bowen. I immediately went to speak with her and thus this connection produced the chance to work with Sandra and her teacher F.R. "Nick" Nocerino (passed away in 2004) who is still considered the foremost expert on the Crystal Skulls.

Through Sandra and Mr. Nocerino I learned about other Crystal Skulls in the world, had a chance to meet some of them. We even teamed together to write a book called "Journeys of the Crystal Skulls Revealed" which is basically out of print now but was published at the end of 1988. During the time I lived within the San Francisco area that began my path to dedicate my life to study of the crystal skulls.

To make a long story short, I have had an opportunity to not only spend time (and sometimes do a type of scientific-paranormal research) with such crystal skulls as "The Mitchell-Hedges Crystal Skull of Love" (the current guardian Bill Homann), "ET" (a single piece human sized dark smoky quartz skull discovered in Guatemala in 1906 and now in the hands of the van Dieten family), "Max" (larger than human size – single piece clear quartz skull in the hands of Joann Parks who was told this skull comes from Guatemala), "Windsong" (larger than human size clear quartz skull purportedly discovered in South America which holds the consciousness of an ET being with the Petri family) and "Synergy" – a larger then human size clear quartz skull also purported discovered in South America, now with Sherry Whitfield). In 2001 I had a chance to meet "The Amethyst Crystal Skull" again in San Jose, California where its current name came out from the research we conducted. Let me explain.

In 1999, I was contacted by one of the businessmen who had "The Amethyst Crystal Skull." We became very good friends. Through his efforts, I was able to return to San Jose, California, with a few friends in the fall of 2001, to not only see this crystal skull again but to conduct a special type of research which utilizes a Meridian Stress Test System that was supplied by my friend Maggy Fox who traveled with us. This device has the ability to record the energetic effect upon people (our test subjects) who were being exposed to this amethyst crystal skull. Sandra Bowen also participated in the experiments. However, after I and a few friends had to leave the Hotel where we stayed during our visit and conducted the research, Sandra did a private session with this crystal skull. It was during this session that the name of the amethyst skull came out and was revealed which was "Ami" that means "friend" and this is how this crystal skull is known today.

The results of our tests showed the following:

First we blindfolded each person being tested so that they would not know what they were being tested with (nothing – called a baseline reading, a piece of amethyst quartz - the same material as "Ami", or "Ami" herself). We did not do these three tests in the same order for each person. The reason for this was so our test subject would not know which item they were being tested with. The Meridian Stress Test System produces a reading of the values from 0 to 100 and takes measurements of various meridians in the human body by touching an electrode to specific meridian points (linked to an organ or system in the body) that reside on a person's hands and feet. A value of 50 is considered total balance of the meridian being measured – a value from 45 to 0 is an illness or low energy in the body and 55 to 100 is a tension or pressure.

Since all of the measurements taken were numeric we could compare the numbers. Basically we could see how the quartz crystal and "Ami" affected the energy meridians in a person body against their normal state or the base-line reading. When "Ami" was introduced the readings either stayed the same or improved (moved towards balance) 90 percent of the time. The quartz crystal made of amethyst only showed about a 65 percent improvement. These figures were consistent with other activated crystal skulls we have worked with as we have our experiments with people in the U.S. or Europe.

It is interesting to note that in 2008, when everyone was going crazy around the Indiana Jones film that involved a Crystal Skull, I was interviewed for a special documentary done by the SyFy channel at Bill Homann's house. While my interview did not air in the final version of this show, we were able to arrange a testing of the Mitchell-Hedges Crystal Skull, my personal 10 pound Smoky Quartz Skull known as Portal de Luz ("Portal of Light") and a piece of clear quartz.

Once again we implemented a Meridian Stress Test System with 7 test subjects of which a member of this group was Mr. Homann. We saw a similar result with improvements in the readings of the test subjects when the new carved skull of Portal de Luz or the Mitchell-Hedges Crystal Skull was introduced but the Mitchell-Hedges Crystal Skull was the most powerful as the energetic enhancement it gave to our test subjects continued past they were put in the presence of this very old skull. One day I will publish these results.

Thus I can say through my exposure over the years with some of the very old crystal skulls discovered in the world, I have felt my own personal energy greatly expanded, uplifted and heighten. However, I am also a co-guardian with my partner Katrina with a set of 17 personal Crystal Skulls which range in size from a small marble to a human sized rose quartz skull which has a separate jaw like the Mitchell-Hedges Skull done by a master carver in China. We also have an old Skull found in the ground in Mongolia when they were building a dam and an Opalite Skull that was aported through a trance physical medium we know in the Seattle after channeling the master Krishna. But most of the personal skulls we have are of modern design. But even with these newer crystal skulls we have also had some profound experiences.

We have witnessed once a crystal skull discovers their true guardian, these skulls somehow acquire a living consciousness that emanates from inside of them. Each Crystal Skull therefore tells us their name, which is a representation of the type of energy they channel and the service they offer to people they meet.

Through our conversations with our personal skulls they sometimes make a request of us to take them to certain locations they wish to visit or a type experience they wish to have. It feels as if we are having a conversation with a real live person. Katrina hears a distinct voice that comes from each skull and I hear them in my mind's thinking voice as I know the thought that entered mind wasn't one I was thinking about. The Crystal Skulls will communicate with you using the spiritual gift or gifts you have that are the strongest.

Now it may sound crazy to think that a Crystal Skull could speak with you but during an interview with our friend Teresa who is a trance medium, an ET spirit made a comment about this. This extraterrestrial being told us that they will work through the Crystal Skulls as a communication device to impart special information and knowledge we can understand. Think about this, would it be so strange to have a head that looks like a human to speak with?

However, Katrina and I are not the only individuals who are having these dialogues with the skulls. There are many people who have contacted us via email tell us they have the same experience with their own Crystal Skulls.

In conclusion, when it's your time to become a guardian or caretaker of a Crystal Skull, be ready for your life to be changed forever. Once a Crystal Skull has integrated with the energy of its guardian they seem to project outward an aspect of this person. This does make a bit of sense as a human being is really an energy being deep inside so the skull can absorb the essence of their guardian. The Crystal Skulls also seem to know how to assist their guardians – what is this person's strengths and weakness – they will mirror back the essence of the person including the aspects which the guardian may not wish to see and finally, the skulls becomes a catalyst to take the person toward their life's destiny.

The following statement comes from soul wisdom – the Crystal Skulls were initially gifted to humanity as a special tool to assist mankind to remember who we truly are as divine children of God (Creator). But as civilizations came and went, humanity slowly forgot its divinity. The most powerful Skulls were hidden or went into other dimensions. Duplicates were created that did not have the energy or power of the older Skulls.

Now the Crystal Skulls are coming back and returning as a sign of the coming transformation of our world. There are a number of theories about how perhaps a set of 13 so-called Original Crystal Skulls will eventually resurface publicly to guide us into a higher vibrational frequency state. To move forward into a time where we can all live together in peace and harmony with those people living on the surface of the earth, with those living underground (hidden or the inner surface of the earth) and with our extraterrestrial visitors.

Get your own newly carved Crystal Skull. See what experiences happen to you. Feel free to contact us with your questions or how to find and/or use your Crystal Skull.

Our book - A Journeys of the Crystal Skull Explorers: Travel Log #2: Search for the Blue Skull in Peru by Joshua Shapiro and Katrina Head – go to http://www.v-j-enterprises.com/CSE-TL2-BlueSkull.htm.

In Peace and Light always,
Joshua Shapiro and Katrina Head,
The crystal skull explorers

Email: http://www.crystalskullexplorers@gmail.com

Website: http://www.crystalskullexplorers.com

CRYSTAL SKULL 1

AKASHIC RECORDS QUESTIONS:

What questions do we ask Skull 1?

Do we follow the Moon Cycles of Jamie Sam's book or just go with numbers 1 to 13?

Ask for the Wisdom of Skull 1 through to Skull 13 and the significance of each number.

The Number One is the Beginning.

I am Skull Number One because I bring forth the Wisdom of the Ancients that is the Foundation of Knowledge, Wisdom and Healing of each of the 13 Skulls.

As Crystal Skull 1:

- I AM the Earth and Heaven, bringing Heaven to Earth through the Trees and Plants
- I Teach Humans how to cultivate and find Food from the Living Earth
- I Teach How to Build Shelter from the Earth's resources
- I Teach the Basics
- I Teach the Foundation - all answers are in the Crystals and microbes in the Earth's Telluric Realm
- I Teach that All Plants have their Individual Function, Purpose and Intelligence
- I Teach that All Trees have their Function, Purpose and each has their own Intelligences as they grow for hundreds of years naturally
- I Teach that the desecration of the Forests is the desecration of vast Libraries of Knowledge of the People of the Stars
- I Teach that it is time to bring forth the changing information that both The Akashic Records and The Crystal Skulls have. (We are using the medium of crystal skulls because you can acquire 12 and work with

Master Homan for the 13th. The Skull he guards is Crystal Skull 13 for Healing and Transformation (humans aren't there yet)

- I Teach the Relationship of All Things – Each having their individual Life Cycle that supports the Whole, while interacting with each other from the smallest microbe that creates Soil from fallen trees and plants
- I Teach that Trees provide Food for All Beings whether one cell or a Being with trillions of cells
- I Teach Survival – I, Crystal Skull Number One, bring forth the Energies to Earth that are needed in each Age – for the Earth and the Heavens are ever Evolving and Changing, just as Humans need to Evolve and Change for Survival of the Species
- I Teach Sufficiency and Sustainability – Living in Harmony with the Earth, herself, and all of the plants and animals.
- I Teach how to work with the Soul of each individual Being
- I Teach How to Bring forth the unique talents and skills of each Being that can be offered in exchange for what we need as a individuals and as groups to survive
- The weakness of Man is Arrogance. MAN = All Humans
- I Teach that Humans have vast intelligence, but none as great as the Living Crystals, Rocks, Trees and the Microbes. I, Skull Number One, Am to share this vast knowledge for the Healing of Aberrant thinking around scarcity and fear. The resources of the Earth, if not desecrated, will provide enough for each Being in each Individual Life Form to live their natural Life Cycle without the violence of greed and war
- What say you, Skull Number One about the Elements of Air, Fire and Water – For you have been speaking only of the Living Earth – The Fourth Element?
- I Teach that Air is the First Element of O_2 (Oxygen) and CO_2 (Carbon Dioxide) then we add Hydrogen to Oxygen to get H_2O (Water) – The East and West. East = Oxygen and the West = Water. The Fire comes from the Sun North/South depending on the Hemisphere. The Poles are shifting and melting from Solar flares. Each Element was necessary to create The Earth. The Fifth Element is the Ether "soul/Spirit." The Life Force Energy that is infused in each living Being whether microbe or the mountain of granite or a 1,000 year old tree, or Man, including the fungus, bacteria and viruses. Each has a purpose and function that is necessary for the balance and homeostasis of the Earth and Each Living Being.

There was no separation among any Earthly Kingdom. They all spoke and communicated with each other, supporting and nurturing each individual Being / Intelligence.

What we are really speaking of is NOT separate life forms but different Intelligences that manifest as Various Life Forms. All of whom have been sad and lonely without their communications with Humans. They miss the Respect, Compassion, Trust, Gratitude and Generosity that once existed filled with patience for each separate Life Cycle. And the Kindness that comes with Respect for the variances and differences.

The communication is through the Heart not the Mind. The separation of the physical body from the Soul and Spirit created by religion has desecrated the ability of the Intelligences to support each other and communicate as they did in the beginning.

We are going back to the beginning to communicate from the Heart. This is the Transformation of Evolution.

SHAMANIC JOURNEY QUESTIONS SKULL 1:

Show us the Energy of Skull 1 please.
What Information does Skull 1 have to share, please?
How do we communicate that Information?
What is the Sound of Skull 1?

SOUND:

The Sound of Skull 1 is the Wind – a gentle breeze rustling through the trees and strong gusts of off shore winds. First there was the word.

ENERGY:

- I AM the Swirling Bright White Light of the Life Force Energy, the Primordial Substance of Creation.
- I AM Androgynous – Speaking for both the Masculine and Feminine in each Being. "Men" will understand me.
- I was created in the Beginning as the Earth cooled.
- I Am a swirling Heart Chakra.
- I AM the Love and Serenity that exists with Communication through the Heart with each Being and their Attributes.
- I exchange Love and Information by focusing only on the gifts of each Being / Intelligences.
- I maintain Balance and Homeostasis with Skull 2.
- I work with All of the Elementals and Elements and All Living Beings.
- I AM the Spark of Life in Each Being / Intelligence – This common Spark Allows and Facilitates the Inter-Communication of Species.

This is how "Shamans" or Indigenous Medicine People control Weather and eliminate Plagues within their common communities. The bacteria and viruses from other regions and areas of the Earth wreaked havoc on Native populations. The Shamans could not communicate with what they did not know existed outside of their Region. They did not have time to learn before everyone was sick and dying. Those that survived learned how to communicate with these new Beings / Intelligences to their Region.

We are pre-programmed for specific geographic locations. This is where we communicate at the "Higher Levels" with the Earth and Heavens with the most accuracy.

In other Regions there is comfort in Remembering past lives there, but the Accuracy of the content is not there. Because of your heritage with Europe and the Arabian Peninsula and the Middle East and Africa with people of Color and Asia for Oriental backgrounds – From the DNA of each Individual there is a connection to other parts of the World. It is different and less accurate because you are not there on the Earth. The communication is the most Accurate where you were born and have lived, in the United States, East of the Mississippi River where it lush and green with four seasons; one Season for each chamber of the Heart.

The Heart of the Earth emanates from the Great Lakes Region. You were born within the Energy of the Earth's Heart Chakra.

That is why you learned to communicate through your Heart.

All communication from this point on – in Journeys and with the Akashic Records will be Heart to Heart.

MORE QUESTIONS and ANSWERS:

How does the Information we received today show us the Talents, Gifts and Abilities of the Feminine?

It shows you the CREATRIX. There is a big bang when something new is created – when a microbe makes a grain of soil or sand. We have spoken of the gifts that each Intelligence has; as these Intelligences are Remembered and brought forward then you and Marlene will create something New because of your vast Wisdom from lifetimes.

More important, however, is your willingness to work with other Intelligences without Judgment (this is true for all Beings).

It is important to stay out of Judgment for you both to bring forth the most accurate information, some of which neither of you has any experience. This is a new affair of the Heart that will allow you both to learn and grow in unimaginable ways at this time. We are so pleased that both of you showed up and said yes.

The other Intelligences are yearning for Communication. You call Skull Uno "She". The word "she" "her" are Feminine. The Feminine Energy Creates. Men, by activating their hearts and acknowledging their Intuitive Selves, can also create.

You and everyone that reads your words are being asked to Learn a New Language of The Heart that you will share one person at a time.

What are the Ancient Teachings of THE SISTERHOOD with regard to Skull Number One?

You are working together with Marlene and other women and this leadership style teaches others by example. Demonstrating how women working together create family and community for the Survival of All of the Intelligences, for the highest and best good.

- Women find or create solutions.
- Women communicate with the various Intelligences.
- Women don't go to war.
- Women don't fear when coming from their Heart.
- Women know that they will always be provided for.
- Women know survival is real if their Hearts are open to new ideas. Women know Communities will survive by working together.
- Women know creating solutions for themselves, their families, their friends and their communities is what changes the reality for the better.
- "Women" is a collective of a vast store house of Wisdom and Creativity gathered over the Millennia – An unspoken "Sisterhood."

In Lynne Twist's Book the "The Soul of Money – Reclaiming the Wealth of Our Inner Resources" there is story of a group of Women Living in the sub-Saharan Desert that was encroaching on their villages and water supply. With no water there is no life. These Women of Senegal came together as a collective to ask the Hunger Project for help. They needed equipment to pump water. They greeted the Hunger Project Team in Celebration with singing and drumming. Lynne Twist was the Leader and after listening to their story, the Senegalese were given the equipment and the women dug the wells in their villages, providing water, providing continued Life and survival. This is the power of collective, cooperative effort for the highest and best good with Appreciation and Gratitude.

The women knew where the water was and asked for assistance. This is Sufficiency and Sustainability. These Villagers didn't have to move to survive.

There is much work around "SISTERHOOD," the collective cooperation for sustainability and survival. "Third World" countries understand this better than the "developed" nations. Technology of computers, cell phones, microwaves, television plus trains, planes and cars have created much separation from family and community and yet can connect us worldwide.

How many of you live where you were born? Each person is ideally seeking a higher wisdom and the higher vibrations of Love that so that they can create a community and live where they are rather than "Running."

The Religious Missionaries advanced the Separation and continue to do so with their "judgments." Science is just coming to truly understand that there is No Separation – Intelligences are everywhere in millions of forms.

"The Sisterhood" pre-Inquisition knew how to hold the multitude of Intelligences and bring them together for the highest and best good of All. "The Sisterhood" holds the Light and Love Steady so that the Masculine can perform the necessary tasks as directed by "The Sisterhood."

The Constitution of the United States is based on the Iroquois Nation Confederation where the Women directed the men and voted. The U.S. Constitution didn't allow women to vote until 1920 under Woodrow Wilson.

The Masculine Characteristics manifest in both Men and Women and The Feminine Characteristics manifest in both Women and Men. It is about Honoring the Unique Gifts, Talents and Abilities as recognized by "The Sisterhood."

The Human Brain is Whole.

Left Brain = Linear Thinking = Masculine Doing = Spring and Summer

Right Brain = Circular = Feminine = Intuitive, Creative = Fall and Winter

43

The Western Culture of The Middle East, Europe, The United States, Canada and Australia has only honored and focused on the linear. The Round, Circular Feminine intuitive has been negated.

Now is the Time for both the Masculine and Feminine living in Harmony and Balance. Women need to empower themselves to Remember to teach their sons and daughters Wholeness and Quantum Thought...

A Thought Changes Everything.

Now is the Time!

CRYSTAL SKULL 2

AKASHIC RECORD QUESTIONS:

Are we to call forth the Elementals, Fairies and Earth Spirit's that want to work with us?

Work with MAP on your own time and those Beings that resonate with you. How does this relate to the 13 Skulls?

The Nature Spirits are always working in Partnership with the 13 Skulls. The 13 Grandmother Skulls represent the Divine Feminine. There is NO Divine Masculine without the Divine Feminine. Love is the key. LOVE of the Earth and All Women thus Creating Balance on Earth. Love Creates Sustainability and Sufficiency for All beings. Each Being fulfills their Purpose in contribution to the Whole.

TRUST IN THE PROCESS OF LIFE

What are our questions for today?

Please refresh your Akashic Records and talk to Skull 2. The Earth information will come through each succeeding Skull. Each Skull has separate yet overlapping information for keeping the Divine Feminine Sacred and how to work with each of the millions of Intelligences to Restore the Balance – The Balance of All Things – The Wisdom, The Power and The Love.

What Energies and Teachings does Skull 2 bring forth?

The Energy of Skull 2 is a bright swirling orange radiating out in all directions. She is the Skull that works with Creation – Life and Death of various species, but more importantly new plants and new microbes that are to specifically heal the Earth.

The Earth is a LIVING BEING – Ancient beyond imagination. Once again, as MAN perpetuates the destruction of the Balance of All of the Earth's

Systems (The oceans, the seas, lakes, rivers and wetlands and the oxygen in the air) and Life on Earth. New Beings need to be created within the Earth for homeostasis – the volcanoes and storms. The Earth is shifting for survival which creates the need for All other species and Intelligences to shift to maintain their own homeostasis.

The Schumann Wave of Gaia has increased from 7.38 Hertz to 7.83 Hertz. People have weakened Immune Systems because they are not in alignment with the increased frequency. Walking on the Earth barefoot and drumming are two of the ways to increase our frequencies and immune systems.

What are the specific Teachings of Skull 2?

- I Am the Creatrix
- I Am the Connection to All Celestial Beings
- I Am the Communicator – sending out the call for assistance to The Universe to maintain homeostasis.
- I Am The Keeper of Balance
- I Am the Skull of Lemuria
- I Am the Land
- I Am the Volcanoes
- I Am the Avalanches
- I Am the Blizzards
- I Am the Snow
- I Am the Hurricanes
- I Am the Tornadoes
- I Am the Floods
- I Am the Rain
- I Am the New Grass
- I Am the Wind
- I Am the Trees
- I Am the Forest Fires
- I Am the Mountains
- I Am the Landslides
- I Am the Oceans and Seas
- I Am the Gulf Stream
- I Am the Pacific Current
- I Am the Ring of Fire
- I Am the Coral Reefs
- I Am the Whales – Keepers of the Records of Earth
- I Am the Dolphins
- I Am All Sentient Beings
- I Am the Birds

- I Am the Bees
- I Am the Eagle and All Raptors
- I Am the Elementals
- I Am All Plagues, Viruses, Bacteria, Parasites, Fungus, and Microbes
- I Am the Destroyer
- I Am the Maker
- I Am Always Flowing – Creating and Destroying
- I Am the Creatrix – Keeper of the Balance
- I Am the Communicator with All That Is

SHAMANIC JOURNEY QUESTIONS:

What Knowledge and Information do you, Skull 2, have for us?
Please tell us about Lemuria before the fall.
What is the Energy of Skull 2?
What is the Sound of Skull 2?

SOUND:

The Sound is the Sound of the crackling fire

ENERGY:

As I look at the Glowing Orange Energy of Skull 2, shimmering Cooper or rusted iron in color and anatomically correct. I hear her say:

"The knowledge I share is the Information for All Ages! Information and Knowledge can NOT be informed without LOVE!"

As the Creatrix and Destroyer – Keeper of the Balance, I can only do my work from a place of deep, deep unconditional Love for the Earth and Her survival as a Living being. I will destroy All Humans before I allow the Earth to die. She is the most precious jewel in the Galaxy.

The Earth can always be re-populated once she has recovered from the neglect and unconscionable destruction of Her systems from greed.

The Oil is for internal Balance which dissipates with its removal

The Gold, Silver and Cooper conduct, attract and send out Energy signals. These elements are Her nervous system, Her electrical system. The Crystals, Precious Jewels and Semi-precious Stones that are mined for their healing

47

properties and their physical beauty cause vacuums in the earth's infra-structure. This creates instability in the foundation of the matrix.

The Earth will re-generate and Heal without Man. Man was to learn to Love and Honor All Beings and Intelligences on Earth. Lemuria came about to give man an opportunity to Keep the Balance on Earth out of Unconditional Love for All Life – Let me repeat All Life.

The Achuar, aka the Shuar or Head Hunters of the Amazon knew this and still do. When the missionaries came there were 7,000. Today there are 70,000+. The Medicine Men and Wisdom Keepers say the Forest has suffered greatly without the Balance that they maintained. For the men had to kill another person for every five grown children he produced to keep the balance. With the population increase the balance is being destroyed.

The Achuar are the last vestiges of Lemuria along with a few Indigenous Cultures hiding deep in the Amazon River Rain Forest, the Lungs of The Earth with the Forests in the Land of the Sami, Siberia and North America.

The Kogi still live in seclusion, keeping others out of their territory, maintaining the Knowledge and Wisdom of the Earth Balance.

The Inca learned the Energy of Gold and then the Greed of Gold. Their Prophesies sent them into hiding 500 years ago with the advent of the Fourth Pachacuti and the arrival of the Spaniards. Their reason was to preserve the remaining Wisdom, and Power available through the Heart Center of Love.

In the late 1990's and early in this Century they came out of hiding to Teach their Wisdom and came to North America to Teach their Wisdom.

It is the time of the Fifth Pachacuti.

The Prophecy of the Marriage of the Condor and the Eagle is as old as the Earth Herself down through various cultures. It is the Marriage of the Intellect/Technology of the brain/ego with the Unconditional Acceptance of All Beings through the Love of The Heart Center.

This Marriage is the 18 inch journey from the Head to the Heart and in some cases from the Heart to the Head for Balance of the Being.

There are many people in The Great Lakes Region that have had the privilege of studying and learning with these people, Ipu, Cleicha, Alberto Tatzo, John Perkins, The Tomayo Family and others who left their home to travel in

48

groups to Teach. I had the privilege of studying with them to learn "Shape shifting" and experiencing their healing techniques.

My husband and I hosted two gatherings on the Eastern Shore of Lake Michigan called "Healing Waters" with Ipu and Cleicha on the Equinox of September 2001 after September 11 attack and again in 2002.

In 2001, we had 500 people on the beach doing ceremony on the 90 percent electropiezo crystal sand with Ipu and Cleicha in a huge circle. I was standing next to Ipu drumming for him when he asked me if I knew what I was doing. I said yes, drumming for you. He laughed uproariously and said No Marilee that isn't what you are really doing – this is community Shamanism. You gathered these people and you are drumming.

Skull 2 continues by saying the Survival of Mother Earth is paramount! I will do anything to insure Her survival, including destroying and creating anew. I, Skull 2, work in conjunction with Grandmother Moon and we work in partnership with the Earth to keep the fluids of Earth and Your Bodies moving. The tides change daily. There are seasons of flooding and draught. The blood of women is released monthly to nurture the Earth or a child for 9 months. That is the Flow – girls growing from infants to adolescence to begin bleeding (releasing blood) to create a new garden ready to be planted/impregnated then birth, growth, harvest and death. It is the Cycle of Life for Humans and for all Mammals.

Birth and Renewal is ONLY POSSIBLE with the FEMININE, who can create life independent of men – There is Immaculate Conception. It has happened before to Restore and Maintain the Balance."

I Am Skull Two (2)

- I Am the Connection to All Celestial Beings/Bodies/Intelligences
- (Stars, Star Systems, Central Sun, Planets and Galaxies)
- I Am the Communicator
- I Am the Creatrix
- I Am the Destroyer
- I Am the Keeper of Balance

CRYSTAL SKULL 3

AKASHIC RECORDS:

Upon opening the Akashic Records, I was directed to use Numerology for the Skull Numbers and their significance. Do Research as you are guided.

The Number 3 is of Importance:

The number 3 is a Triangle – It is the Foundation with 1 and 2.
It is the first building block – It is the first closed form – a solid as it were. Now we add God's Geometry – Sacred Geometry which includes the plutonic solids.

The Triangle represents Mother, Father, Universe (All That Is)
The Triangle represents Spirit/ Soul, Body and Mind
The Triangle is Mother, Daughter, and Holy Soul
The Triangle is Father, Son, and Holy Spirit

Two Triangles = a Square
Two Triangles = Philosopher's Diamond* or Star of David (Hiram's Symbol)

*Numerology and the Divine Triangle by Faith Javane and Dusty Bunker, Pg. 44 – ISBN 0-914918-10-9; Whitford Press, a division of Schiffer Publishing, Ltd. 77 Lower Valley Road, Atglen, PA 19310, USA

AKASHIC RECORD QUESTIONS:

What are the Job, Purpose and Significance of Skull 3?
What specific Wisdom does Skull 3 bring forth?

SHAMANIC JOURNEY QUESTIONS:

Show us the Energy of Skull 3?
What is the Healing of Skull 3?
What is the Sound of Skull 3?

SOUND:

The Sound of Skull 3 is the Sound of Water:

- A babbling brook
- The crashing waves
- The rushing water of river rapids
- The breaking of ice
- The Snow Falling in Winter and on the Mountains
- The gentle Rain Fall, cleaning and nourishing.

HEALING:

Skull 3 is the Healing and Wisdom of Feelings and Emotions. All Creatures have feelings and highly accurate Senses. Diamond, your dog, is very sad when you leave the house without her. She KNOWS LOVE, as do all of the Infinite Creator's children. It is from Emotional Pain that Lower Frequency emotions come into play. Emotions are not limited to Mammals. The Trees cry when they are damaged – the sap is their tears sent to repair the wound. With so much pollution, Trees are having hard time breathing.

The Feelings and Emotions of All Beings and Intelligences are the Wisdom that I, Skull 3 bring forth. Without Emotion and Feelings there is no passion or intention to manifest or materialize.

Think about the Life Cycle of Flowers that brings all of us Joy, Healing and Food.

ENERGY:

The Energy of Skull 3 is a swirling energy of Luminous Golden Light of Love.

- I Am a bright sun bringing warmth to All.
- I Am the Laughter of Abundance.
- I Am Faith.
- I Am the Yearly Cycles as the Earth Circles the Sun.
- I Am the Movement of the Tides of the Waters as Moon Circles the Earth.

The Energy is a Circle of Light Twirling and Swirling in an ever expanding procession of Light.

I Am the Energy that brings Mother/Father; God/Goddess that creates together in an explosive Orgasm aspiring to reach the Heart Center of the Universe that emanates all the beautiful attributes of Love:

- The Grace
- The Gratitude
- The Trust
- The Forgiveness
- The Responsibility
- The Respect
- The Kindness
- The Compassion
- The Generosity
- The Hope
- The Honesty
- The Joy
- The Patience
- The Happiness
- The bliss
- The Leadership
- The Non-Interference
- The Courage
- The Charity
- The Dedication
- The Praise
- The Self-Love
- The Thankfulness
- The Unconditional Acceptance
- The Unconditional Love

The Healing in the Plant and Animal Kingdoms is automatic. They are also Teachers. We are now learning from the Elementals and Microbes, too, who are also Healers and Teachers.

The Animals with their specific attributes have always been teachers, guides and protectors in the Human Journey of Oneness.

Like the Skulls 1 and 2, I Am Skull 3, who teaching integration of the high fine frequencies and essences of Love. By loving the wounded Soul we are Healing of the Past, Present and Future. The Emotions manifest Wounds. With Intention, this brings about Healing and the return of Oneness.

That is why in any Culture "Soul Retrieval" is so important a Healing Modality for Humans. The Trauma can be healed with Loving Intention, bringing forth and returning the higher vibrations and essences of Love from the energy field (aura) to its rightful place in the body.

The Healing of Skull 3 comes from the 3. As a triangle, I Skull 3, work with the Celestial Realms and the Sun to bring Healing Light to Earth with the Knowledge, Power and Wisdom of the luminous Golden Light.

On the Earth Plane, ALL "dis-ease", stress and discomfort is from missing Light Frequencies and the Vibration of Sound in the Human Body. Without the Harmonics of the Life Force Energy, Humans and Beings and Intelligences wither and die. That is why life spans at this time on Earth are much shorter than genetically possible.

Genetically, within our DNA, we can live to be 120 to 140 years of age naturally when connected to Earth with a constant flow of Golden Light. Each of the Seven Generations will be known to each other with women having babies in their 70's with no degenerative diseases (cancer, heart/cardiovascular disease, diabetes, HIV, lupus, arthritis, etc.). The Elders live vibrant lives with Full Mental Capacities, Eyesight and Hearing.

I, Skull 3, bring forth the Healing Modalities, of Reiki, Dar'Shem, Deeksha, Healing Touch, Quantum Touch, Laying on of Hands and Hands of Light. Healing also comes from sending the Healing Golden Light out of the Heart Center into the World, raising the vibration of those near and far, operating at the Quantum level.

I Am Skull 3. Skull 3 is the Keeper of the Healing Plants, which also operate at the Quantum level. The blood of the plants as therapeutic essential oils, oxygenate, raise vibrations of the entire body they are applied to that raise the vibration of Humans and Animals with their frequencies. Each plant will heals a specific issue or issues spiritually, emotionally and physically.

If the Spiritual/Emotional Complex is not dealt with, the Stress caused the emotional/spiritual wounds sinks deeper and deeper into the energy field and then deeper and deeper into the physical body causing what Western Medicine calls disease.

The Physical body, below the head, is the Super-conscious that knows all. It is that part of the body where the Heart resides. The Human Body – Your Body – will never lie to you. You and All Humans can learn the Language of your body and its signals. When you learn the subtle signs and symbols and

See, Feel and Hear the Subtle Energies around you carried in the luminous Golden Light all around you and in you. You and All Humans will begin their Re-Connection with the Earth and All Her Creatures, plants, trees, animals, insects, birds and the Beings and Intelligences of the Inner Earth.

The Parietal Lobe of the human brain is that part of the brain that shows us special arrangement (the height of stairs, placement of furniture, the space between objects, etc.). The parietal lobe is over loaded deepening the Human sense of space and separation between individuals and the millions of Beings and Intelligences of the Inner and Outer Earth Plane.

The Ego, home of human Fear, lives just below the parietal lobe of the brain. This area of the brain is the verbal mind and is the size of a golf ball. The Verbal Mind only knows the language of its culture and the fear that separation creates.

As Skull 3, my purpose is to help re-integrate the Lobes of the Brain and the Hemispheres so that spatial arrangements are possible while feeling a part of the WHOLE ALL.

All Skulls are like your computer chips – All Skulls are Intelligences, not artificial intelligences. The Quantum Biofeedback Machine you call SCIO (To Know) in Intelligent and an Agent of Change by giving the person the frequencies they need to come into homeostasis.

AKASHIC RECORDS:

The Akashic Records guided me to re-do Skull 3 because there was more information and I was given these questions:

What say you regarding Skull 3?
What is the relevance with Gaia Matrix Oracle and Numerology?
What is the relationship of the Numerology of the Skulls and our work?
What is the significance of the colors of the Skulls?

The following is the information that I received from the Akashic Records:

Skull 3 is about Emotion. Intention comes from Emotion and Passion of Love.

The 3 is a Triangle the first solid shape. The Triangle represents the Trinity.

Three (3) is the Holy Trinity of:

- Body, Mind, Spirit
- Soul, Spirit, Being
- Mother, Father, God (Creator/Universe)
- Mother, Daughter, Holy Soul
- Father, Son, Holy Spirit

All of the Trinities exist within Each Being. It is your relationship with yourself and with your Healing – your creation, your lessons; your wounds are for your healing or the healing in the moment.

The Trinities represent the Ascension process of the return journey to Source the Cosmic Heart of Infinite Love. In Native American Culture this Journey is around The Medicine Wheel – The Cycles of Life, The procession of the Sun (Seasons of the Year) and Moon (months).

There is a Trinity of three times around the Medicine Wheel – Each complete Circle is at a higher vibration than the time before.

In finishing this book I was guided to look and learn more about triangles exist in the Medicine Wheel. How many triangles are in the Wheel of the 13 Crystal Skulls?

Also I'll talk about the Caves of the Ancestors that live in each direction. The Caves of the Ancestors can be found in Part IV. This is information that came to me after sitting with the M-H Skull of Love on December 6, 2012 – The beginning of the Mayan Celebrations for The Shift.

In section IX there are additional pictures of the Mayan Medicine Wheel. The colors align with the Woodland Nations of Indiana, Michigan, the Algonquin Nations and the Apache of Arizona. East is Red; South is Yellow; West is Black and North is White.

North = Earth: Skulls 4, 8 and 12, Color is White - In the Southern Hemisphere this is Summer

East = Air: Skulls, 1, 5 and 9, Color is Red

South = Fire: Skulls 2, 6 and 10, Color is Yellow – In the Southern Hemisphere this is Winter

West = Water: Skulls 3, 7 and 11, Color is Black or Blue

Center Inner and Outer Circles:

The Center Circle is 13, the Whole Healed Medicine Wheel. The Skull 13 lives here and is Love, the Transformation - the Center of Creation. Each direction and each element has significance and is related to the Skulls and their numbers.

Each quarter or quadrant or triangle is 13 years and the whole is 1 representing O + 3 the triangle = 4 the Building Block. First is the Triangle 1 +2 = 3, the Triangle.

The Skulls are aligned with their number. Three (3) is a triangle. One/1 is Circle

The Circle - The Sun is a Circle; The Earth is a Circle; The Moon is a Circle.

The journey of the Moon around the Earth is a Circle – with 13 Moons per calendar year. With the Medicine Wheel we start in the Center at O and move to the East and around the Medicine Wheel and End at 13, the completely healed Medicine Wheel functioning at the highest vibrations for the highest and best good of All. This is when the All will be able to receive the Guidance, Wisdom, Healing and Visions of the Skulls for the Earth's Survival.

The Skulls are the Earth's messenger system. The Silver/White; Orange/Cooper and Luminous Gold of Skulls 1, 2 and 3 is the Electrical System of the Earth and Humans. It is the Kundalini and Meridians, another triangle of energy.

The colors have a numerical correspondence that supports the number. Each color has its own frequency and essence.

The Numerology is everything because each number and each combination of numbers have a specific vibration. The Skulls correspond to the Esoteric Numerology of the Kabala and the Norse Tree of Life as well as the Gaia Matrix Oracle by Kryder, PhD.

The Skulls are Teachers, Healers and Recording Devices, each with their unique individual frequency.

Skull 3 is about Emotions and bringing forth the highest, finest Essences, the Essences of Love the highest vibration in the Universe. The Love Vibration is necessary to heal the lower vibrations of wounded and negative emotions and thoughts.

The Love Vibration is necessary in Each Being for our Survival.

JOURNEY OF A CRYSTAL SKULL CARETAKER
By: Linda (Allayah) Frisch, New Jersey, USA

Marilee, I appreciate the opportunity to share my crystal journey and insights on the Timeless Ones commonly known as Crystal Skulls. I have intuited that crystal light energy is a conscious light form that was seeded into Gaia by the EL's-the shining ones during pre Lemurian times. This light consciousness works in a symbiotic alignment with all Gaia's light/life forms, for their spiritual consciousness development. Thus the term-Timeless Ones- as this exceeds all timeline definition imposed by mans' understanding. All crystal life forms are connected to the Infinite Source.

During this special time of service, my spiritual journey is unique to me yet reflective of many incarnated souls. I incarnated as an awake and aware soul. As a very young child I re-experienced many past lives and heard and saw multidimensional visions and star beings. I closed down many times in my life to fit in this world. Ultimately, this caused an imbalance in my higher chakras and a deterioration of the health of my physical vessel. In 1999, I had a very serious surgery-a massive benign tumor on my brain stem—seat of the soul entry. I experienced a Near Death Experience (NDE) during the intensive care period after the surgery.

A soul decision was made. The Allayah aspect, who worked with the crystalline beings descended and integrated. The journey began through synchronicity. I was able to reclaim many ancient relics and timeless crystal skulls. I know they are part of my ancient soul in many lifetimes and are here for the ascension into the New Earth Star.

Presently, I watch over and care for just under 20 ancient skulls, both quartz and jade, and numerous ancient energy tools and relics. Many of the relics and ancient skulls reflect the energy of the Divine Mother Consciousness. They are physical representatives of that energy integrating into Gaia during this cycle.

The Jades I have intuited hold the energy of the Pleiades. They connect to many indigenous teachings. One of the ancient Jades has a turtle on its brow.

It was shared that indigenous oral folklore stated that four turtle bundles would be sent to Gaia from the Pleiades for the shift of ages according to a respected Elder. I have three of these turtle bundles which have been used in ceremony in areas such as serpent mound—this work was done privately.

My White Tara Skull arrived with her dark over coating. My dear shaman friend cleaned her. The powder, tested by a university, is tree resin. The three ancient Himalayan Quartz Skulls in my guardianship work as a sacred trinity of triangulated energy. White Tara holds the Divine Mother Energy, Melchizadek holds the Patriarchal Energy and White Dove holds "Christos", the Holy Soul/Spirit Energy.

The ancient Himalayan Skulls have gained recognition by Hopi Elders and others as true Lights. One of these skulls is now guarded by Mayan elders. These Himalayan skulls have found their caretakers and are located all over the world now. Their guardians are doing the healing and Earth Keeper work they incarnated to do.

My first ancient or timeless skull came to me through synchronicity. I had a modern carved Canadian polar Jade Skull carving-simply called Jade. She came to me in dream time and showed me how to create an energetic portal using sacred geometry configurations with specific crystals I was instructed to gather. When created I was told to connect the lines with a laser quartz wand then place Jade in the middle and pull the lines up to an apex or pyramid shape with her as the cap stone and to say a mantra that was not familiar.

Shortly thereafter I reconnected with Frank Loo, who was instrumental in my having these jades and Skulls. Frank Loo is a very knowledgeable collector of jade artifacts and we talked about ancient jade. One day he asked if I would be interested in an ancient jade skull with a turtle on its head and its companion jade turtle. I just said yes... they came from an estate collection in Nepal.

Prior to the jade skull's arrival, I had hundreds of black birds in my front and back yard... I was to realize every time an energy piece came here its arrival was announced by a flock of black birds gathering in my yard...

When I open the box and took the skull out- I clearly heard the name Earthstar. All this was so new to me... I then placed this jade skull in a spring rain to clear and cleanse, I felt a sigh. When I brought it in I heard inner sounds of drumming and felt or saw a journey into a dense rainforest of the Amazon... I was guided to ask an indigenous elder clairvoyant I know to read this skull.

As explained above, the folklore legend of four turtle jade turtle bundles being sent down by Pleiades to be re-emerged for the shift. Earthstar was one with its companion turtle was one of the bundles. In time I reclaimed three bundles in total.

After a few months Frank contacted me to ask if I would be interested in an ancient quartz skull. It was from the group he called the Himalayan skulls. I had very little knowledge of crystal skulls at the time, yet felt I needed to reclaim them. I immediately said yes even wondering why I felt I had to. Frank Loo said he would be sending one to me. Now this was sight unseen! Talk about blind trust.

Legend states that certain Crystal Skulls from Atlantis were covered in a resin to hold in their bright light when they were hidden until the time for them to re-emerge. My White Tara Skull is one such Skull. She arrived with her dark over coating.

While White Tara was on her way to me, I had very profound experiences. I felt her way before she arrived; a gentle subtle energy. First I would get whiff of flowers. I narrowed the scent down to either roses or jasmine - it seemed to alternate. Then one day I suddenly received a vision of a white skin Asian girl with colorful makeup. Nothing made sense to me because at this time I had no recent knowledge of Buddhist or Asian history. At other times, I would see her and began to hear a lilting voice, a young Chinese woman almost a sing song voice. She announced I am the White Tara. I knew that was to be her name. I contacted Frank Loo and asked if I was given the name for the skull white Tara who was the White Tara. Frank said it was perfect and proceeded to tell me that she was divinely selected to be returned to me. Frank had a deeply spiritual side to him at that time. White Tara's return to me was prophetic in a way I cannot deny or explain.

During this time of pre-arrival, I had other visions in color of the Mother Mary and smell the fragrance of roses. Then a vision of Isis standing before me in full color and Kuan Yin, another goddess I soon became acquainted with energetically. It took me awhile to figure out the meaning of these visions of female deities from many cultures. This Crystal Being connected to the Mother ray of Source. Within her I find the Divine Mother energy.

With impending delivery, I had amazing manifestations. Periodically my back and front yards were literally covered with hundreds of blackbirds chirping. Then as suddenly as they appeared they disappeared.

On the day she arrived--I was looking out the door as Frank said she was due. I saw two people in my driveway dressed in brown uniforms--so non-descript except their skin was BLUE!!! Then they nodded at me. I was shocked; I looked again and they were gone. I started to doubt myself but in my heart I knew what I saw blue skin people in my driveway. I rarely share this story but I feel it is time for people to recognize the Tara and her purpose. Because I was so shaken by my vision, when the doorbell rang, I was afraid to answer it, not knowing what to expect. It was a regular UPS delivery man with my Skull.

The box containing her was hot to the touch. As I opened it, I was hit with a wave of energy that causing my neck to tighten up and take my breath away. In my head I heard a quiet sigh as if she was glad to be returned to my hands. This is my experience. I could never have made this up.

So White Tara has arrived and the journey begins... The Tara energy has continually guided me to get involved in the internet sharing her words and starting groups for those who seek to understand. And the journey continues with the internet connections listed below.

The role and responsibility of a crystal skull caretaker is to work in a symbiotic union, to allow and to express the unique energy of the light consciousness streaming thru the timeless one for the higher good of all life on this planet. For example, as a human being whose soul aspect is connected to the Divine Mother's, I am their physical voice. The female alchemist of Love energy works with the spoken word. The Skulls communicate with me thru vision and clairaudience; Words to Heal; Words to Inspire; Words to Facilitate Personal Growth.

The energy of Crystal Skulls is Timeless. Humanity as evolving crystal beings are drawn to the Skulls as they are Light Portals for access their own Akasha for self-growth.

The Skulls started our journeys anew in the present. We feel the tugging of our Soul to regroup with these Crystal Libraries. They are the Timeless Ancestors connecting with the Hearts of the Rainbow People.

Hear Your Song
Follow Your Heart
Time is Now
The New Earth shines brightly
Heaven meets Earth

So the journey of the work of the crystal skulls continues into the Now and Beyond; People connecting with like-minded folks, coming together in groups in the physical or on the Internet. Human Beings are aligning their energies in circles of heart communities in service of all life forms. All inspired by the portals of light, with the wisdom, knowledge and understanding of the Crystal Skulls.

The journey we make into the NOW begins with our awareness of our crystalline light body integrating into our own physical body. Our perceptions have now shifted and we have merged in a symbiotic oneness with All Life/Source. From this stance we are in contact with the universal mind of crystal consciousness and can extend this perception thus creating a link between the crystal skull consciousness and our light mind. We now see and experience the two consciousness's' simultaneously; Oneness is achieved. What I have learned from this experience is that the solidified crystalline light form we call a crystal skull is US. The crystal library that holds all of the records of the "I AM" within and waits to be integrated and expressed.
Marilee asked why I love the crystal skulls. I love them as I am learning to love my own energy that they show me. The veils are lifted so that awareness is revealed. Our purpose for incarnating during this time can continue. The Akasha of All That Is of our own light is contained in the crystal skull libraries we draw to us.

Linda Frisch

http://www.sanctuaryoftheancients.com
http://www.facebook.com/Allayah

CRYSTAL SKULL 4

AKASHIC RECORDS:

What say you regarding Skull 4?
What additional Information is there to be shared?

Skull 4 is the cube, the second solid form. The Four (4) is the number for the Earth. The cube is two equilateral triangles put together and becomes the foundation of all "building blocks."

This is where Energy becomes Matter/Mater/Mother.

The crystalline structure of the Earth is a Cube.
The crystalline structure of Salt is a Cube.
The crystalline structure of Humans is a Cube.

This is where the saying that "Humans are the salt of the Earth" came from.

Energetically, Salt repels all negativity and cleanses. Meat was preserved with Salt. Salt was put around houses to repel unwanted energy.
The Oceans and Seas are Salt Water as is the Water of the Woman's Womb. These two waters are exactly the same and nourish Life.
Salt from the Seas contains all of the minerals that Humans bodies need to thrive. Minerals are the building blocks of the human body and are the same minerals found in the Earth.

Silver/White is Nature's antibiotic mineral.
Cooper/Orange facilitates the flow of energy – relieving pain.
Gold is needed for the brain to rest and process information.

The conscious mind one (1) cannot produce. The subconscious mind, two (2), cannot reason. It takes 1 and 2 to produce emotion (3) which leads to manifestation and the orderly progression to four (4), the organization of the conscious elements. Four corresponds to the Earth.

Looking down from space and to our Galaxy, the Earth is the precious blue sapphire jewel of the Universe. The Blue and Green of Sea and lush Land complement and support each other. Emerald Green complements the Sapphire Blue at their highest vibration. All Blue, green and blue green stones, both precious and semi-precious are for healing as they bring the Earth to us to harmonize our energies, especially turquoise, malachite and Chrysocolla: The Peace Crystal looks like the Earth.

Chrysocolla is a very beautiful stone with much beneficial energy. Chrysocolla is a stone of peace, increased wisdom, and discretion. It promotes level-headedness, encouraging clarity of thought and a neutral, cool attitude during turbulence. It can be used to decrease nervousness...

Stones and rocks are foundation stones for structures of all kinds, from caves to adobe, to brick to granite or marble buildings and facades. The Stones and Bones of the Earth hold the history of the planet.

Number 4 is the builder. It is $2 + 2 = 4 = $ Two pairs. It is a family of four where all things are possible. Four is the perfect combination of Male and Female Energy for the first time.

Masculine Energies of East and South = Air and Fire

Feminine Energies of West and North = Water and Earth

The Medicine Wheel is whole and balanced for the first time, The Circle is complete.

SHAMANIC JOURNEYS:

Please show us the Energy of Skull 4.
What Information does Skull 4 have to share?
What is the Sound of Skull 4?

SOUND

The Sound of Skull 4 is the Sound of the Earth, Wind, Fire, Water, Birds chirping and singing, the trees talking, the night sounds of the animals, frogs, of the cicadas, raccoons, coyotes...

ENERGY

The Energy of Skull 4 is Red Jasper for the Earth and root chakra and the heart. It is family and community. Its higher color is Zoesite – raw emerald and ruby combined in swirling green and pinky/red. At the highest vibration it is a beautiful Diamond, the Master Healer and builder.

The number four brings visions for a better way of living. Where there is cooperation and sufficiency and sustainability.

Number Four is where there is communication with the heavens as demonstrated with the cube foundation of the pyramids of the Egyptians, Mayans, Aztecs and the Mound Builders of the Midwest in Southern Illinois at Cahokia.

The energy of a Diamond is a transmitting and receiving station. The highest quality crystals of computer chips are a lower frequency than diamonds. Diamonds are used to cut because they are so hard as well as having a very high vibration. A Diamond is a Master Healer the feminine aspect of the shape and number 4. All women are Healers.

A Cube, as pictured, is the masculine aspect as a "building block."

All men are doers/hunters/ builders.

Crystal Skull 4 has this to say about its teachings:

- I Crystal Skull 4 teach Family Building.
- I Crystal Skull 4 teach Community Building.
- I Crystal Skull 4 teach Cooperation.
- I Crystal Skull 4 teach Organization – Council of Elders sitting in Circle.
- I Crystal Skull 4 teach Organization Building.
- I Crystal Skull 4 teach structure of groups in human societies, in the microbial kingdom, in the plant kingdom and in the animal kingdom.
- I Crystal Skull 4 teach Accomplishment through the Organization of Tasks. I am in a Bee Hive, an Ant Colony, in the growth of a tree or a plant. I organize the tasks of the microbial kingdom, including, bacteria, funguses and minerals.

Wolves are an example of some of my best work on how to organize and work as a community for survival. (As I observe man's ignorance, I am appalled at the killing of wolves because they do not understand that they are the "balance keepers" of Nature, only providing for their families. They don't kill just to kill for sport as man does from helicopters.)

64

- I Am Crystal Skull 4 the Center of Your Human Body.
- I Am the Four Chambers of the Heart.
- I Am the Crossroads of All flowing Energies.
- I Am the Center where the Light of the Universe meets the Love of the Earth in the Human Heart Center.
- I Am the Receiving and Giving Center.
- I Am the Number for Shamans and Medicine People of the Earth - Earthkeepers.
- I Am the Planting and the Harvest.
- I Am the Builder.
- I Am the Balance.
- I Am the Healer.
- I Am the Four Elements of the Earth, working together in cooperation.

The reflection of number four heals. Skull 4 heals as a crystal and provides the basics–Food, Shelter and Clothing.

For an Abundant Life Spiritually, Emotionally, Intellectually and Physically – Honor the Four.

Thursday – March 3, 2011 - The Day before the New Moon.

My Akashic Records:

On this day before moving on, immediately upon opening "My" Records as guided, I received guidance to research and include information on the Platonic Solids before moving on to Crystal Skull 5. This is exciting for me because I love learning, research and geometry – I am in heaven. The information below is the result of my research in a condensed form.

Doing research for this book led me to this website, http://www.crystalwind.ca and is the resource for some of the Plutonic Solids information plus information from "Numerology and the Divine Triangle," my favorite book on numerology.

PLUTONIC SOLIDS – THERE IS A PICTURE IN SECTION X:

Sacred Geometry – The Plutonic Solids are three-dimensional shapes that have equal sides, angles and faces. They demonstrate the overlapping sciences of physics, philosophy mathematics and theology.

History is unclear about who discovered Sacred Geometry – whether it's Pythagoras or Plato is unknown. My intuition is that Pythagoras made the intriguing discovery and analysis. Platonic Solids are a set of five, three dimensional, shapes that date back to the Greek mathematician Pythagoras and later named after the Greek Philosopher Plato.

The Tetrahedron, Cube, Octahedron, Dodecahedron and Icosahedron each have unique characteristics, in that the sides, edges and angles are all congruent. In other words, all sides are equal, the angles are the same and the faces are identical.

It was the great Greek Philosopher, Plato, who paired each of the platonic solids with a classical element (fire, earth, water, air, and ethers/Universe). He believed that these three dimensional shapes were the building blocks to the creation of everything in and around us.

If you view a 3-D model of any of the elements contained in the periodic tables, you will see that each has a crystalline structure at the Atomic level made up of these Platonic Solids shapes.

The Five Plutonic Solids are: Picture in Part X

Tetrahedron – The 3 sided Pyramid – The Solar Plexus
Hexahedron – The Cube = 6 sides – The Base Chakra
Octahedron – The 8 sides - Heart Chakra
Dodecahedron – 12 sides – The Third Eye
Icosahedron – 20 sides – The Sacral Chakra
Star Tetrahedron Merkaba – Sacred Geometry of three Tetrahedrons

TETRAHEDRON- (THE PYRAMID) has three sides and is associated with the Solar Plexus, the seat of Emotion in the Human Body. Tetrahedron relates to the Purpose of Skull 3.

This is the first and simplest Solid object with four sides and the first Plutonic Solid – the Triangular Pyramid, the Fire Element which relates to Skull 2.

HEXAHEDRON – (THE CUBE) is associated with the Base Chakra and naturally corresponds to Earth. It is stable. It is the basis for western architecture and salt crystallizes into cubes. The six faces naturally link it to the planets except for the sun, which is the center.

The Cube is the second of the five shapes. It contains six square faces, 8 vertices and 12 edges. The Cubic Shapes are found in the natural structures and natural formations of many crystals, including Salt, Pyrite, and some Fluorites. The Cube is the Earth Element and Skull 4.

OCTAHEDRON – (Diamond: 2 to 5 sided Pyramids-the base is the fifth side)

This is the third plutonic solid in the series and is associated with the Heart Chakra. This form represents the merging of Spiritual, Emotional, Mental and Physical planes, thus symbolizing a state of completion.

The double Pyramid of the Octahedron is a key factor in reaching Oneness or Enlightenment. The great pyramid of Giza is reflected underground with a complex of 23 temples representing the 23 stars of Orion. The Diamond represents our Earthly–Celestial Connection.

The Octahedron is made from placing two square based pyramids base to base. The naturally occurring crystals that exhibit these properties include: Fluorite – green, white, clear and purple on colors.

Magnetite – the most magnetic of all the naturally occurring minerals.
Diamond – The hardest of Stones and the Master Healer.
Octahedron corresponds to the Element of Air for Skull 1 and Skull 8 for the Diamond shape with 8 sides.

On the Medicine wheel this is East for Air and Earth for North and the position of skull 8.

DODECAHEDRON – (Pentagon – 12 sides)

This Plutonic Solid is number four in the series with 12 pentagon faces, 20 vertices and 30 edges. This Solid along with the next shape is the closest in shape to a sphere or Circle.

The Pentagon is the Center shape of a five pointed star – the star of Venus that can be found on many flags in the Middle East. Venus rises before the Sun. Each side of the Pentagon is said to represent one of the Plutonic Solids or the Five Elements of Earth Air, Fire and Water and the Fifth Element being Ether – The Living Life Force Energy of Creator.

This Plutonic Solid has 12 sides – 12 is a Sacred Number with many connections to Art, Music, Literature and Spirituality. It has been of Spiritual and Metaphysical interest for millennia. Like gem Crystals, it pulls our eyes and heart in to observe more deeply, gaining insights, knowledge and wisdom. It has been said that the Dodecahedron represents an idealized form of Divine thought, will or idea.

Dodecahedron corresponds to the Element of Ether, which is Skull 5. This also corresponds to Skull 12. Again, the Skulls are in the East position on the Medicine Wheel for Skull 5 and North for Skull 12.

ICOSAHEDRON – (20 sides of Equilateral Triangles)

This is the last in the Series of Plutonic Solid shapes. This shape is made from 20 Equilateral Triangles; it has 12 Vertices and 30 Edges. Notice the correlation to the Dodecahedron with 12 Triangles; 20 Vertices and 30 Edges. The Faces and Vertices number are reversed. This shape is also very close to being a sphere.

This shape represents movement, flow and change. This form is found in Nature in various viruses. This Sacred Geometry offers help in balancing the Emotions. As a Homeopathic it can help eliminate Viruses, facilitate the regeneration of the physical body with its Healing Energy that calms Emotions thus reducing Stress. When we reduce the Stress we create an environment that kills the viruses restoring homeostasis to our emotions, mind and body.

Icosahedron corresponds to the Element of Water, which are Skulls 3, 7 and 11.

March 4, 2011- The New Moon AND Sacred Geometry

These Plutonic Solids work with two-dimensional Sacred Geometry as well as their three dimensions. The two-dimensional Sacred Geometric Shapes are:

One (1 - vertical line) and – (horizontal line) everything else comes from these forms.

68

+ is an Equilateral Cross and surrounded by a Circle is the shape of the Medicine Wheel. The Center is the starting point moving to the East then around the wheel back to East.

The Circle represents the Godhead; Creator; All That Is; Spirit; I Am; Love, because it enfolds and contains; it maintains its shape; it is justice because it is always in perfect balance. A circle is the Alpha and the Omega – The Beginning and The End. There are 360 degrees in a circle = 3+6+0 = 9 = completion.

The 2-D Triangle is a horizontal line with 2 vertical lines tips meeting to form a solid shape. The triangle has 3 – 60 degrees angles for 180 degrees = 9.

The 2-D Square is 2 vertical lines and 2 horizontal lines and is complete with four 90 degree angles = 4 x 90 = 360 = 9 completion.

All other shapes are a combination of this foundation.

The Star of Venus (the five pointed Star) has a pentagon in the center and represents five. The Pentagon represents Freedom, Inner Hearing/Knowing, Intuition, Change and Mental Growth. Five is the number of the Five Senses; the Five Elements in the diagram above, Ether/Spirit, Air, Fire, Water and Earth.

What Does the Five Pointed Star Symbolize?

The five-pointed star can be found in many places, from the night sky in a child's drawing to representing ancient world religions. Likewise, what the five-pointed star symbolizes changes drastically with each culture's interpretation, and its significance has followed the course of human history for thousands of years.

The Facts:

The five-pointed star, commonly called a pentagram, consists of an unbroken line crossing to form five points. Commonly, one point sticks upwards, while two go left and right and two stick out from the bottom. The pentagram can be circled or not. For some, the lack of a circle represents the star's awareness or activity level being high, while circled signifies protection, and connection.

Pagan Beliefs:

In some of humanity's oldest belief systems, the five points of the pentagram represent the five earthly materials: the top being spirit and the other four being earth, air, fire and water. Thus, the inversion of the pentagram supplicates man to his carnal nature, since spirit, thought to be man's godliest attribute, sits below the more material substances. In addition, the pentagram was sometimes associated with Mars, symbolizing harmony through conflict.

Other Religions:

For other religions, the pentagram takes on entirely new meanings. For Muslims, the five points may correspond with the five pillars of faith or their five daily prayers. For Christians, the five points correspond with the five wounds of Christ. Later in the Christian tradition, the five points symbolize the virtues of a medieval knight as exemplified by Sir Gawain: generosity, courtesy, chastity, chivalry and piety. However, later, the cross overtook the pentagram as the primary Christian symbol. Ironically the pentagram is now often viewed as a pagan and evil symbol by some Christians because of the work of French occultist Eliphas Levi in the 19th century.

General Symbolization:

• Da Vinci's Vitruvian Man

In a broader sense, the pentagram symbolizes features of humanity in general. This can be seen in Leonardo Da Vinci's Vitruvian man, whose extremities can be mapped to the pentagram. In addition, the five points correspond to the five digits on each hand and foot, the five senses, and the categorization of human life into five stages: birth, adolescence, coitus, parenthood, and death. 5 pointed Star Corresponds to Skull 5.

History:

The history of the pentagram can be traced through many ancient cultures. The symbol was used in the 4th century BC in Mesopotamia. The Druids thought of the pentagram as a symbol for the Godhead, while in the 12th century the Knights Templar associated the symbol with Christianity. The pentagram may have had a hand in the design of the pyramids, since for the Egyptians; the symbol was associated with the underworld.

Six pointed star is formed by two intersecting equilateral triangles. It is called the Philosopher's Stone; Hiram's Symbol; the Seal of Solomon or the Star of David. It represents the balance of male and female energies and marriage and family. This symbol also has 360 degrees with 6 x 60 degrees = 360 degrees = 9 completion. Corresponds to Skull 6 and diagram can be found in Part IX – pictures.

The Vertical V shaped triangle is Mother at the lower point, upper-right point is Daughter and the upper-left point is Holy Soul. This is matter made manifest on Earth.

The other Equilateral triangle is Father at the upper-point, the lower-left point is Son and the lower-right point is Holy Spirit.

Two Dimensional Geometry stops here and we work with Sacred Geometry.

NUMEROLOGY:

First, I must tell you that I love numbers and Numerology for they hold the frequencies and vibrations of the Universe and Multiverse. I once owned a business called Vibrational Healing. It is fun to see the inter-connection of all things with numbers, geometry, plutonic solids and sacred geometry...I am still so very excited about all of this coming forth when it is so needed.

As we meet with each Skull we will discover the deeper meaning. We will learn the why of Each Skull the assigned purpose of each specific number. Numbers are the Key to the Universe. Each Number and each Combination of Numbers has their own unique frequency and vibration. Every living Being has a Vibration and Frequency. Human DNA holds keys to the Individual and Each Being has their own Akashic Record based on their frequency and vibration.

Sound (First there was the Word) and Light are the only two sources of vibration in the known Universe and on Planet Earth.

Seven (7) is an open vertical line attached to a horizontal line at the top left of its point. Seven is a principle number in the Old Testament as a day of rest.

The Lord's Prayer has 7 lines/stanzas. It is 3 + 4 or 5+2 or 6+1 and is indivisible.

Eight (8) is two circles – one on top of the other = As Above, So Below, As Below, So Above – the ever flowing energy from the Universe to Earth and Earth to the Universe – Ideally each one reflecting the other. When the (8) is on its side it is called Infinity.

Nine (9) is a circle with a vertical line attached to its right side 9 is completion, it is the last single digit number – The End.

Ten (10) – New Beginning = 1+ 0 = 1 supported by the Godhead/ Creator. We start a New at a higher vibration, blazing a new trail supported by God; Source; Creator; All that Is.

Eleven (11) equals Transformation – a steady flow of Energy down the column creating change for the highest and best good. 1+1 = 2 and is written 11/2. This number is about partnership with All that Is. We are now in partnership after started anew.

Twelve (12) is 1 + 2 = 3 at a higher vibration. 12/3 is the Accumulation of Courage, Wisdom and Presence of Mind for Preservation. The Wheel of Life has been traveled three times and The Medicine Wheel is complete.

Peace and Serenity and Freedom are key words for this number and have been earned through trials and tribulations of the other numbers of The Zodiac Wheel of Life. This is the ever flowing Waters of Life from the Heavens.

Thirteen (13) = 1 + 3 = 4 = 13/4 is Death and Re-Birth in a Non-Ordinary Sense. Change as the Cycles of Life Changes with each of the 13 Moons in a calendar year along with the each of the four Seasons. We are born; we turn 13, the end of childhood a death as it were. This is the end of what no longer serves. Thirteen = Change, Release, Transformation.

ZERO (0):

The Number Zero (0) was recognized by the Mayans and Olmecs. They understood that 0 represented No -Thing and Everything. It was symbolized with an Oyster shell.

Number Zero is The Circle, The Medicine Wheel, and The Void of All Creation.

The following information is from:
http://www.TheDreamtime.com regarding the Interpretation of 0:

Zero means Null, Nothing/Everything, The Void, The Circle, Hollow, Empty.

Astrology: Zero = the Moon (symbolically), ruler of Cancer, Emptiness, spiritual essence, nothingness, blank Emptiness that contains everything.

The Essential Void, Zero, Derived from the Latin 'nulla figura' (not a real figure). Zero is relatively new in terms of mystical symbolism, except that it is not.

Ancient Mayans and Olmecs had a basic understanding of the concept and represented Zero as an empty oyster.

We can look at the Oyster as a giver of life and therefore Zero as both an empty, hollow form but also a form which produces a living being and by adding a grain of sand, another being almost magically produced called a pearl, another orb.

Character Traits:

Empty yet whole, the Essence of all things, accepting and creative with the addition of the Zero from the Mayan Culture – we have an added dimension to Ten (10). The Zero is the Center of the Medicine Wheel and the Outer Ring – Nothing and Everything with thirteen years for each quarter = 52 years total.

When a person reaches their 52nd birthday it is said in Native American cultures that they have walked the Medicine Wheel and have the honor of being called Grandmother or Grandfather.

We have 13 Moon Cycles per year and the Elements of the Medicine are the annual turning of the Moon around the Earth and the Earth around the Sun. As explained earlier the Four Elements are Earth, Air, Fire and Water – But ETHER is the Fifth Element.

Zero is the beginning and the end; the Alpha and the Omega and is – The Energy of All Things where the duality of our world disappears until we choose it.

The Skulls are Quantum – The Quantum Healing of Non – Locality.

The Crystal Skulls operate at the Quantum Level by transmitting without being physically present in our space. I have a small Rose Quartz Skull that was always present in our Sacred Space. We added a small blue Sodalite Skull in April, 2011, now Called Blue Rose, thus expanding the energy.

On March 5, 2011, I listened to Amit Goswami of International Quantum University of Integrative Medicine. The subject was Gifts of Quantum Physics to Natural Medicine.

He spoke on the Quantum Healing and the practices of the Indigenous Peoples of the Americas, including South America, North America, Canada, Alaska and Hawaii. He explained how they live a Quantum Life of Possibilities. Their concerns are not for the Material "Things" but of their well-being and connectedness to All That Is.

The Quecha language of the Q'ero people of the Andes of Peru and Ecuador makes no distinction between "Pachamama the Earth and Pachamama the Universe."

From my experience and study of Shamanism, the Sami People of Northern Norway and Sweden work in the same way as do most indigenous cultures that have maintained their connection to the Earth.

Shaman is a Russian word meaning "Medicine Person" who recognizes that there is only "dis-ease" where there is a "Wrong Mental Meaning" causing blocks thus causing disease.

Healing is staying in the Creative process. The Crystal Skulls bring Healing by giving us insights and "correct mental meaning" of how things truly work so we can heal ourselves, our families and our friends. I am reminded of this continually, especially as I write. I just received another healing three days ago that has made it easier to complete this book as I do the final run through.

The Skulls are Quantum Healers by transferring information and insights for "Ah-ha" moments to further our understanding of the Universe we live in. The Skulls are a Gift from the Universe for the Evolution of mankind.

The Mayan Calendar is about evolution of 26,000 years. You ask "What has this to do with numbers of the Skulls and this Age and the Medicine Wheel?"

They are related and are to teach us a way of being that connects us to each other and all of the Natural World on Earth and in Space.

It is a Gift whose Time is NOW!

ETHER is here – the fifth element is the unquantifiable life force in the empty spaces. It is neutral! There is no right or wrong, good or bad, no feminine or masculine, no light and dark.

ETHER is represented in Skull 5 and is creating infinite possibilities and choices. We will get to this when we finish Skull 4 after this long interruption with information needed for clarity.

Friday, March 4, 2011 – (The New Moon from the dark void comes all creation. We do our Journey Drum Circles on the New Moon)

Question:

What additional Information do we need from Skull 4?

Research more, research Mayan Prophecies of the 13 Crystal Skulls; Learn from Carl Calleman regarding the Mayan Calendar Prophecies; go back to the Barbara Hand Clow book "The Mayan Code"

Keep working on Numerology and Sacred Geometry. You are getting good information when you are quietly receiving. It is time to share your ability to make things understandable for the many, not a select few.

Skull 4 is about the Four Elements and how they work together. Get clear that the 13th Skull is the Beginning and the Ending – It is the Center of the Medicine Wheel. Number 13 is the Primordial Ooze that is in the Beginning and Death. It is directly related to the Mayan Calendar and Numerology and The Zodiac – The Cycles of our lives.

Skull 4 is about Matter and Manifesting.

My question:

How does Skull 4 work with Emotion?

Emotion is Skull 3 and the Third (3rd) Chakra. If it is any color other than gold; golden yellow or bright yellow, the highest Intention will not be made

75

manifest for the clouds surrounding will block love and the loving passion to bring it forth.

The Skulls each emanate different aspects of Pure Unconditional Love. If that Love from Creator and Mother is blocked in anyway – there is no ability to hear or receive from the Devic Realm, the Earth, The Heavens, The Animals, and The Plants. Without Love, our inability to receive from other humans is magnified. Sharing becomes difficult and fear sets in manifesting as anger, depression, greed, jealousy and many other lower vibrating feelings and emotions.

Skull 4 is unable to manifest or support the manifestation of the higher essences and ideals if the Emotional Energy is clouded with heart woundedness from childhood that has not been healed.

How do the Skulls facilitate the healing of this woundedness?

The Skulls raise the Vibrations and Frequencies around them which automatically raise the individual's frequencies. They can be a part of any MAP Team. MAP is Medical Assistance Program and is Quantum Healing.

The Skulls want to disseminate information so that people/Humans can take responsibility for their own wellbeing and health and not look to Western, Allopathic Medicine and Pharmaceuticals for a quick fix.

Once we the people take responsibility for our own lives and how we spend our money, we will start to heal by slowing down. It is very important for humans, and for the impact our on the Earth, to slow down and do more with less with a knowing that each person can heal themselves.

March 2011 I listened to an online class given by Dr. Amit Goswami, Quantum Physicist of The Secret. The class was on "Quantum Healing and Indigenous People" and sponsored by the International Quantum University of Integrative Medicine.

According to Dr. Amit Goswami, author of "The Quantum Doctor," Quantum Physics provides us a model that proposes consciousness as the underlying reality, the ground of all being, the basis for a deeper understanding of the universe and the functioning of the art of healing.

In Western Medicine and Science, Causation is upward, which is why only the symptoms are addressed rather than consciousness. The Gifts of Quantum

Physics to Medicine, according to Goswami, are Non-locality, Tangled Hierarchy, and Discontinuous Leap in Consciousness.

The Quantum paradigm of "Consciousness is the ground of Everything" is reflected in the fundamental principles of "All My Relations", "All things are part of All things", and "Everything is part of me and I am a part of Everything" found in the Native Hawaiian, Alaskan and Native American traditions.

Dr. Amit Goswami and Dr. Paul Drouin discussed the Gifts of Quantum Physics to Natural Medicine and how Quantum Healing relates to Native Healing. Native Peoples of the Americas understand the Unity of Heart and Mind to be able to unleash the Healing Power of Consciousness. This was a part of their way of living – living a Quantum Life of Interconnectedness not bound by locality, signals and electronics. They know that everything has energy and is transmitting waves.

They know that Creator sends messages to the Brain, which sends them to the Cells which send them to the Atoms, the Molecules, to the Elementary Particles to Possibilities. In the Quantum World all objects are Waves of Possibility.

Causation is downward. Native Americans understand downward causation and live from that perspective with rituals and ceremonies for healing including Drum Circles, Dancing, Powwows, Purification/Healing "sweat" Lodges and Visions quests. All of which we have attended or had on our Land, Sage Spirit Terra which means Healing Spirit Land.

This will be discussed at length in our next book of the Trilogy on Prayer and Meditation.

Prayer and Meditation create an Intention and the Human Brain needs Intention to manifest its desired outcome – There is Downward Causation of Consciousness.

A few experiments have been performed for the Western Mind, which demonstrated that the Brain accepts non-local communication and healing. This is also accepted by Shamans and their Traditions.

The Shamanic way of living needs to be re-established around the world.

We, my husband, dog and I, live a fairly simple Shamanic life by following the natural cycles of the Earth rather than the Julian calendar. We honor all of

77

the animals in our woods and have it designated as a protected area called a Classified Forest – we do much to reduce our carbon footprint. We have no dishwasher, only one car and one TV (which I could live without).

Consciousness chooses without signals because it is connected to all possibilities and is choosing from itself – CHOOSING FROM ITSELF. How exciting to have this ability and we all do if we only slow down to wake up.

That is why Vision Quests produce "AHA" moments and insights that are a surprise and a surprise with renewed interconnectedness - not logical = Quantum Creativity. Quantum Creativity does not track with scientific creativity.

Creativity and Imagination are from the God Source, The Creator and your high self. Creativity is truly continual conscious process and will continue until the appropriate time. Creativity, Imagination and Intuition are in continually moving on the waves of possibility. Yet there are four steps corresponding to the number four 4 – the number for the Earth:

1.) Preparation of space or circle for a Vision Quest;
2.) Incubation – processing.
3.) Insight or Vision the Quantum Leap
4.) Manifestation.

Healing is staying in the creative process and waves of possibility. We make choices for ourselves. We can choose hands-on or long-distance or other modalities of some form. Our modality of choice will support our Intention.

"Wrong Mental Meaning" is also called "Stinking Thinking" in AA Circles. It is what creates "blockages" causing "dis-ease" or stress leading to disease. Shamans can facilitate the discovery of what is producing the blockage. When we recognize the block it goes away. "Soul Retrieval" which is a form of Quantum Healing, performed by Shamans after trauma has been experienced.

With Quantum Healing and working with Nature, Plants in the form of herbs and Therapeutic Grade Essential Oils and Homeopathic Medicine there are no side effects; MSDS (material safety data sheets) are NOT required.

The price of Allopathic Medicine and Pharmaceuticals is a huge price in terms of their very dangerous and deadly side-affects plus the financial burden to individuals and society... They have created their market by creating a need, no serving market needs. There is no natural health management. This economic model of materialism and "stuff" of no longer serves the population. Native Americans know this. Other needs were and are more important.

We need Shamanic Marketing where the Needs of the People are supplied and Individual needs are met. That is not happening for the most part, especially with Genetically Modified "Franken" Food and margarine instead of butter, artificial sweeteners, Corn Sugar instead of molasses, honey, maple sugar and pure unbleached cane sugar. Just ask your liver about the difference between corn sugar and cane sugar.

How do we deliver our message of possibilities without making people upset or angry?

You interface with people from your heart with Unconditional Love and Acceptance.

Some will still get upset, but not to the degree as when they came in the door. If you are on TV, they will change channels or turn it off. They will leave your presence and they won't buy your books.

Opening to who you really are to deliver your message is teaching by example. The process of having a completed published book is a healing process in a safe secure way.

You are opening your hearts and throat and creative center to be who you really are – It is not about other people's opinion. It is about your healing and growth while providing knowledge and services to that the population needs that resonate with you.

Shamanic Marketing will be incorporated and is your marketing foundation. With all of your businesses you have seen a need and filled the void. Entrepreneurs are Shamans – they have a Vision that they make manifest.

CRYSTAL SKULL 5

Friday – March 11, 2011

Today is a 3+11+2011= 3+11+ 4= 18/9 = completion. This is also an 11/11 portal of which there are 12 and this is the third one, supporting the higher vibrating energy of the Ninth Wave of the Mayan Prophesies.

Akashic Records for 3/11/11:

What Say You Regarding Skull 5?
0 and 13 = The Center of the Mayan Cross or as I have been calling the Medicine Wheel.

1 = Air – East
3 = Water – West (Reverse in the Southern Hemisphere for Energy flows counter clockwise in The Southern Hemisphere)

2 = Fire – South/North
4 = Earth – North/South

Skull # 5 = ETHER = East

- ETHER is a New Element truly.
- Ether is an Element of Neutrality without Polarity.
- Ether represents the Fifth Element = the Fifth World = The Fifth Dimension = The Fifth Sun.
- Ether is Spirit.
- Ether is the un-quantifiable Life Force Energy in the empty spaces.
- Ether is Neutral; there is no right or wrong; good or bad; no feminine or masculine, no light or dark.
- ETHER Just Is. Ether is creating the Infinite Possibilities and Choices. It is a very pale lavender in color or light blue of the Fifth Chakra in the throat of humans.
- Ether is in the East on the Medicine Wheel, represented by Air "And First there was the Word".

- In the Quantum World of possibilities Ether is the Consciousness; where Causation is a downward flow of Infinite Possibilities. Which one do you choose?
- Ether doesn't have an opinion or judgment about what you choose. It provides the possibilities for you to choose for yourself.

Skull 5 is located in the East of Beginnings on the Medicine Wheel or Mayan Cross at a higher Vibration. Ether moves with the Wind – Whispering the Voice of the Universe "What do you choose?"

Skull 5 is The Ether, the Infinite Possibilities and Choices.

Skull 5 teaches us to ride the wave of Possibilities and Choices. Do you choose the high vibration choice or not?

Remember in the movie "What the Bleep" there is a scene on an outdoor basketball court and there are many balls bouncing? All of those bouncing balls represented the many choices the main character had. Will she choose the one that makes the basket or one of the other choices – like hitting the rim? In the movie she made a perfect shot into the net.

There is no judgment with Ether. "Judge Not that You be judged."

We are here on the Earth plane to make choices for our Soul's growth and Healing – Thus the infinite possibilities – choices for every Soul. You can call it another step in the Ascension staircase up or down depending on your Vibrational choice.

Five is the 5 - pointed Star of Venus. It is the five sided pentagon. It is the in between shape in Geometry and the Dodecahedron of Sacred Geometry with 12 pentagons, 20 vertices and 30 edges.

Five is $1 + 4 = 5$. In numerology, five is the number for change, freedom, and knowledge. It promotes progress through a willingness to accept change; to adopt new concepts and points of understanding. The number 5 is about claiming the liberty to suggest new ways of doing things with the ability to present the new in logical and acceptable terms. New ideas that promote enlightenment are the key to number 5. New Ideas = Possibilities and Choices.

Skull 5 is ETHER.

Ether is Quantum. Which choices do you make? What are the possibilities?

81

Question – What additional information do we need regarding Skull 5?

- I Am Skull 5 the Hearing
- I Am Skull 5 connected to the human Sacrum and the Earth.
- I Am Skull 5, the voices on the Wind.
- I Am Skull 5, flowing unseen Air, and the downward flow.
- I Am that I Am
- I Am Neutral
- I Am the Word
- I Am Knowledge
- I Am Wisdom
- I Am Skull 5, Infinite Possibilities - I hold "AHA" moments for each being.
- I Am Skull 5, The Transmitting Station of the Universe.
- I Am Skull 5, Receiving infinite possibilities then transmitting those possibilities to You. You must get very quiet to know me.
- I Am the Whisperer –
- I Am the Knowing – Clairsentience
- I Am the Seeing – Clairvoyance
- I Am the Hearing – Clairaudience

The possibilities are ever flowing and changing. Once a person, you, hears, sees, knows or feels the "Blockage" or "Vision" and acts upon it – The possibilities change.

I Am Skull 5 and I tell you this is the way of the Infinite Universe:

- possibilities
- choices
- resonance
- responsibility
- healing/enlightenment
- possibilities
- choices
- resonance
- responsibility
- healing/enlightenment

This is the process on into infinity – The vertical figure 8 with the horizontal infinity sign of the Earth plane.

The throat and hearing in all humans is blocked because of the lies told to you as children and what you have experienced and do experience. Then they are

82

told they are wrong and "don't know" by adults hiding some sort of aberrant behavior. Then the children don't Trust themselves.

Thus the throat shuts down because they can't speak their own Truth as they know it. By shutting down the throat, their connection to their family, their friends, and their community and to the Earth is shut down. This shutting down thus creates fear within the child.

Fear was created when they shut down of their throats which are connected to their hearing, fear of speaking what they heard and saw. When fear occurs, then the children quit playing with their unseen (to others) friends and helpers. They no longer communicate with their animal totems and guardians. The children quit sharing and singing; they are afraid to feel the vastness of their Love.

I Am Skull 5. I am here to heal the Children and the Inner Child in each Being. For all of the Earth's creatures, Beings and Intelligences, including the trees, plants and animals, became very sad without out their friends communication. Separation created the fear, denying the Whole of existence.

I Am Skull 5, I am here to restore that communication and heal the chasm.

SHAMANIC JOURNEYS to SKULL 5:

What is the Energy of Skull 5?
What is the Information of Skull 5?
What is the Sound of Skull 5?

SOUND:

The Sound of Skull 5 is the Sound of Silence – The Voice of the Universe, The Language of Light, of Colors.

ENERGY of SKULL 5:

- I Am pale blue, white and lavender swirling of the Ether
- I Am soft and gentle
- I Am the way of the future that begins Now; Today a portal is open to the infinite possibilities
- I Am a New Beginning that is possible
- I Am Pregnant with possibilities
- I Am Available to those Humans that Slow Down to Ask
- I AM Available to those Humans that Slow Down to Hear/Listen

- I Am Peace on Earth
- I Am war in the everyday cacophony of the media, the multi-national corporations and governments
- I Am the Possibilities Creating Wholeness Within
- I Am the Possibility of Miracles
- I Am the Possibility of True Abundance of Sustainability for Each Being, Creature and Intelligence
- I Am Sufficiency for Each Being blowing in the Wind
- I Am the Ability to Hear and Speak Your Truth – Your Truth, not what has been told to you.
- I Am the Universe/God/ Creator/Source Speaking directly to You.
- I Am the one showing you "Your Truth"
- I Am the one showing you How to Begin the First Day of Rest of Your Life
- I speak with you through the Sky images, the Wind, the Trees, the birds, the animals daily

The possibilities and choices change based on your Willingness. Yes, Willingness to believe in the Quantum World of Infinite Possibilities

Will You Listen?
Will You have the Strength and Courage to Speak Your Truths?
Will You make the Changes Your Soul Requests?

If you answered "yes" to any of these questions –

- I Skull 5 will help you. I will facilitate your Soul's growth with a continual flow of possibilities as you speak your individual truths. It is a Continuum.
- I Skull 5 facilitate the possibility of healing on all levels (physical, mental, emotional and spiritual) when you call in your Medical Assistance Team. It is Etheric Realms. (MAP – Medical Assistance Program created Machaelle Small Wright is Healing from the Etheric Realms. Her books are available via the Internet and bookstores.)
- I Am Mathematics – Albert Einstein listened E=MC2
- I Am Quantum Physics
- I Am Quantum Healing of non-locality – Prayers
- I Am Reiki, Dar'Shem, Quantum Touch, Healing Touch
- I Am Shamanic Journeys as you travel to the drum beat seeking your answers. It is Direct Revelation.
- I Am Shamanic Healing
- I Am Pan
- I Am the Great White Brotherhood

- I Am the Nature Divas whispering on the Wind
- I Am the Ascended Masters
- I Am the Akashic Records
- I Am Guided Meditations
- I Am All Possibilities
- I Am the Whole
- I Am the Unseen Life Force of All Things in space and time
- I Am Skull 5 – a square topped by an equilateral triangle – the whole is neutral – square feminine and masculine triangle as the symbols.
- I Am the Pentagram of the 5-pointed Star of Venus, the Planet of Love.
- I travel the Air with messages, possibilities and choices.
- I Am the Pentagram of Pagans, Witches and Druids and All Earth based belief systems.
- I Am the One speaking to these people who listen to the Winds, watch the Clouds.
- I Am the One speaking to the Shamans who recognize symbols
- I Am the One speaking to those who understand natural healing and non-local healing energy
- I Am Skull 5, the ever downward water fall of Possibilities, Information, Wisdom, Healing, and Choices traveling in the Light and in the empty spaces.

If you choose a possibility that is NOT your Soul's Truth, it won't work.

(I personally speak to this. It was the summer of 2012; I was following the guide lines for marketing my first book. I kept saying "This is the old paradigm", but I didn't listen. I kept pushing myself until Spirit took me down literally. I woke up after the full Moon drum circle on August 2, 2012(Lughnassah) and couldn't walk. My left knee was infected and swollen. As I healed, receiving loving care from my husband and friends while I finished the first manuscript for the Hay House writing contest my knee got better. It took 6 weeks. Now when I am with fearful people or pushing too hard, I have pain. Left knee pain is my barometer.)

When it doesn't work or is truly complete you choose again. Then you choose again until everything starts fitting together like a jigsaw puzzle, and then more possibilities show up.

- I Am Skull 5, the Skull that will help you define and clarify your Soul's Truth and Purpose. Everyone is a "Shaman" "Healer" "Sage".

Another way to say it in our Western Culture is that:

1. Everyone can Hear, See, Feel and Know what appears to them, but that is not available for others.
2. Everyone can Heal themselves by changing their thinking based on the possibilities raining down from space.
3. Share and Teach the Knowledge and Wisdom to those that "Have Ears To Hear and Eyes to See"

In these three stages are the possibilities for your Soul's Enfoldment – You, me, we must continually be aware of the Infinite Flow of Possibilities; be aware of the Choices, of the Resonance, of the Responsibility, of the Healing. You Can Heal Yourself/Soul. Then you can help others and the Earth Mother and All of her children.

Miracles Happen!
Miracles are always available!

The Time is NOW!

Definition of the Mayan Cross:

Definition of the Mayan Cross: 5-point cross consisting these of five signs is the basis for "*Access Your Personal Power Skull*" in Part III...

Center = day of Birth, which defines the Energy each person comes into the World with

Above is the conception sign, the energy under which a person is conceived. Father, Mother, everything the person brings from previous lives, and their family genes are all imprinted at the moment of conception

Below is the Destiny Sign where a person must aim their lives in order to grow.

Right Side speaks of the physical and material side of the person.

Left Side determines the Spiritual and Emotional side.

86

The Combination of all five signs outlines a person's strengths and weaknesses.

In Part IV there are two diagrams of the Medicine Wheel...

CRYSTAL SKULL 6

AKASHIC RECORDS - Questions:

What say you regarding Skull 6?
What additional Information do we need regarding Skull 6?

Skull 6 is the Balance. It is the Sacred Marriage of the Divine Masculine and Feminine.

Skull 6 represents the perfect harmony, balance and equality of the Divine Masculine and the Divine Feminine energies.

Skull 6 is the Intersected Energies of Sacred Sex as represented by the 6-pointed star – Hiram's Symbol. It is the Seal of Solomon created by Hiram Abif, builder of Solomon's Temple as the Chief Architect. It represents balance. It is NOT just a Jewish or Israeli Symbol although it is sometimes called the Star of David. In Sacred Geometry it is the Philosopher's Stone.

The two equilateral triangles form a cube of 360 degrees. See Part IX for a diagram. Each Triangle only has 180 degrees or half of the Whole. The Circle and Cube of Sacred Geometry have 360 degrees. This is the completion of 2 equilateral triangles of 180 degrees each - intersected equaling 360 degrees, 360 is the number of days in the Mayan Calendar. This is the Philosopher's Diamond with 360 degrees.

The intersection of these triangles represents Sacred Sex. Sex = Six. Sex is a term we still use for the intermingling of the Divine Feminine and Divine Masculine.

The Red (Fire) – upward pointing triangle represents the Flame, the Masculine.

The Blue (Water) – downward pointing triangle represents the Womb.
The 6-pointed Star is the Symbol of Sacred Marriage. 3+3=6; 2+4=6 and 1+5=6

The Female Triangle stands on its point, it is Mother; the Upper Right Point is Daughter and the Upper Left Point is Holy Soul.

The Male Triangle with the Upper Point is Father; the Lower Left Point is Son and the Lower Right Point is Holy Spirit.

No point is more important than the other – Each equal in their function and purpose.

Skull 6 is the dancing Kundalini of the Silver and Gold Chords dancing up the Spinal Column – [The Caduceus] Keeping the Life Force Energy balanced and ever flowing. Part XI – picture of Crystal Spine and the 6-pointed star.

Skull 6 maintains the Balance in The Nature Realms as the changes occur adjustments are made – maintaining the infinite cycles of birth and death.

Skull 6 connects the Divine Mind to The Heart of the Earth.

Skull 6 connects the human mind of Humans to their Divine Human Heart

- I Am the Star of Balance;
- I Am Birth as represented by the Center of the Hexagon.
- I Skull 6 Am Androgynous as a completed symbol (360degrees)
- I Skull 6 express the highest vibrations of both Masculine and Feminine;
- I Skull 6 express The Divine Nature of Each. This really is 3 + 3 = The Integrated Energies.

The dance of the First Element and the Fifth Element (Air and Ether) Wind and Spirit in the first place on the Medicine Wheel bringing forth the Quantum possibilities.

Then 2 + 4 is another marriage of Fire (masculine") and Earth (Feminine) the second is Fire and the Fourth is Earth. From this marriage comes Life on Earth – plants and animals.

The Human Body is the Element of Water and Blood. The place of Healing on the Medicine Wheel – It is number 3.

This is the 6-Pointed Star relative to the Human Body

- I Am Skull 6, I Am in every cell of a new born baby created in a Sacred Way with Love and Light.

The number 6 is important and the Sacred Geometry is important .Six is an Arabic Number and if the edges are squared off – there are 6 – 90 degree angles which equal 360 degrees, The Greek Key or the Philosopher's Diamond.

This Six-Pointed Star Symbol represents the Balance that Healers brought forth with the recognition of Energetic Blockages. Cleared blockages bring and restore balance.

Notice that all of the platonic solids have a triangle except the Dodecahedron. Each side of the cube is two equilateral triangles that are not intersected. The Octahedron is the Heart Chakra and no matter how it is turned it is always in balance.

This is because SIX is the number of sides of a Cube, the Sacred Geometry figure of Foundation. SIX is the number of fundamental forces to the ancients.

The six pointed Star is represented on the Earth Calendar every Spring and Autumn – Fire in Aries in the Spring or Vernal Equinox and Air in Libra in the Autumn Equinox.

The Zodiac Calendar has all four Elements in perfect balance 3 of each one:

Aries = Fire = Spring Equinox the beginning of the year in the Northern Hemisphere

Taurus = Earth = May 1= Beltane = Sacred Marriage - Planting of Seeds

Gemini = Air

Cancer = Water = Summer Solstice when the Sun is at zenith.

Leo = Fire = First Harvest of Wheat

Virgo = Earth

Libra = Air = Autumn Equinox and The Harvest

Scorpio = Water = Healing Time and All Souls Day when we honor the Ancestors

Sagittarius = Fire = Winter Solstice when the Light returns after the shortest day.

Capricorn = Earth

Aquarius = Air = St. Bridgid's Day when we wash away the old Crone of Mother Earth to welcome the new young virgin to start preparing for spring planting.

Pisces = Water

There are six masculine signs of Air and Fire and six feminine symbols of Water and Earth. There are six months each of male energy and 6 months each of female energy. Spring and Summer are Masculine doing time of the year balance with the Feminine receptive time of Autumn and Winter with the dance of the elements returning to Equal in the Spring and Autumn when the amount of day and night are the same.

The number six as represented by the Philosopher's Diamond sits in South on the Medicine Wheel at a higher vibration than 2.

Skull 6 is the South on the Medicine Wheel at a Higher Vibration than 2. It is the place of the War Chiefs who are charged with the duty of Peace Keepers. Summer is a time of celebration. They use celebration and contests instead of actual war if possible – This is true for all Nature based societies.

In Numerology the number six as a Path of Destiny number is a Domestic vibration – Home and Family Tree; The Tree of Life. In Tarot, the number 6 is the Lovers and the Astrological Correspondence is Gemini (The Twins).

The Square and Compass has long been the symbol of the Freemasons. It is from Hiram Abif, The First Mason who knew the "Secrets" of Balance in the Life, in Architecture and in the dance of energies of the Divine – The Giving and Receiving, creating a new a new person, a new family, a new tribe, a new state and a new nation. That is the progression as we expand the energy. It has been expanded too far towards the masculine and now is the time of balance.

The Square and Compass of the Freemasons

With the ending of the Mayan Creation Calendar, the paradigm is shifting from Linear to Circular to balance the Masculine and Feminine energies.

Another name of the symbol is the Double Interlaced Triangle of Solomon. It is also the sign or symbol of Vishnu, a god of GENERATION to the Hindu/Vedic Traditions.

The Mystery Schools claim that there was never a real "King Solomon." The word Solomon is to be broken down into three parts:

Sol, meaning SUN in Latin,
Om, a sacred word in Hindu/Buddhist/Vedic traditions also meaning the SUN,
On, the ancient Egyptian name for their city of the SUN (also known as Heliopolis).

The symbol is consisting of two equilateral triangles, one pointed up, and the other pointed down. The triangle pointing up represents FIRE and the MALE principle (dominant, control, make things happen, etc.)

The triangle pointing down represents WATER and the FEMALE principle [submissive, spontaneous, let things happen, etc.]. Thus we say, men are from MARS [FIRE] and women are from VENUS [WATER].

The two triangles together form a SIX sided star. The number SIX is extremely important to the Mystery Schools, who held it to be the number of MANIFESTATION or GENERATION.

SIX is the only number in which its factors are three consecutive numbers [the first three numbers!] which add up to itself [$6=1\times2\times3=1+2+3=6$]. In the Bible, God takes SIX days to create the world, and creates man on the SIXTH day. Even today we use the word "sex" to describe the GENERATIVE act.

Thus, the Seal of Solomon is a symbol of the SUN and its GENERATIVE powers. The bonding of male and female is not meant literally as in sex but metaphorically to represent the universal principle of DUALITY as well as the androgynous nature of the Absolute/Creator (both male and female, fire and water, everything and nothing).

To the Mystery Schools, gender is a quality of imperfection, as by definition, each gender is lacking in something that the other has. In order to create life, it is reasoned that the Creator must have both male and female properties. Anyway, this can go on and on as we can delve into the intricacies of the symbol (it also represents ETERNITY), so for all points and purposes, just know that it is a symbol of the SUN and its GENERATIVE powers.

It is adopted as the symbol of the flag of Israel to symbolize the power of the Cult of the SUN (Mystery School) and the GENERATION of a New World Order.

The nation of Israel is the planting of the seed to disrupt the Old Arabic Order. As stated earlier, the Philosopher's Diamond is not a Jewish Symbol, yet Israel adopted it and it has come to symbolize Israel in this time.

However, this symbol is not limited to Israel. You will find this symbol on the Great Seal of the United States as well. If one pays attention, it will appear in many unexpected places (especially those that relate to the secret societies).

Anyway, that was to show just how deep the meaning behind a symbol as seemingly simple as a hexagram can be.

The purpose of this is to offer a general understanding of the Mystery Schools.

All of the Mystery Schools also taught of an ancient progenitor society that we now know as Atlantis from which all of their teachings (as well as high human civilization/culture) originated.

It was a society of extremely high culture that transmuted other cultures that came in contact with it. Do you see any similarities to our current culture?

Atlantis existed in what the ancients referred to as ancient times, meaning that it was ancient even to them. Atlantis was described to be a place where its inhabitants knew the use of "magic" which some interpret as "high technology". However, their misuse of "magic" was the cause of their downfall, and the city/island/continent of Atlantis was destroyed suddenly in a great deluge, and much of its knowledge and culture was lost (refer back to legends and the preservation of the Light expanding technologies – the Crystal Skulls).

The Mystery Schools believe that they are the preservers of the Atlantean tradition and that the Mystery system originated in Atlantis. They believe Atlantis to be a Utopia and that it is their duty to establish the New Atlantis. This is referred to as the Great Work. Do you believe this? Personally, it is my feeling that this perpetuations the segregation and separation. Where there is separation no one comes in Unity and Peace.

Mother Theresa said *"If we have no peace, it is because we have forgotten that we belong to each other"*. This is one of the messages of the 13 Crystal Skulls stated a little differently.

Some further readings/sources, if you would like to research:

http://books.google.com/books?id=1WB3g0dcJz8C&pg=PA123&lpg=PA123&dq#PPP7,M1
http://www.theosociety.org/pasadena/etgloss/etg-hp.htm
http://www.theosociety.org/pasadena/sd/sd-hp.htm
http://www.sacred-texts.com/eso/sta/

It is important to understand the Mystery School concept as it relates to the "Secrets" where the Truth is only revealed after years of study and initiations. The Roman Catholic Church is a Mystery School with many ancient artifacts housed in the Vatican. The Roman Catholics simply adopted much of the pagan symbolism and built churches over Sacred Wells and on Sacred Sites. The Mayans had "Mystery" Schools in their Priesthood, who held the information very close to the chest. Their deep knowledge and understanding of the workings of the Universe is very accurate and one of the many reasons the 13 Original Skulls have been buried and scattered around the world.

The Time Is Now! It is time to know the TRUTH as revealed by the Akasha and the Skulls themselves for those with Eyes to See and Ears to Hear.

Mystery Schools still thrive today, and their symbols are everywhere. The Mystery Schools were basically religious cults that protected sacred knowledge and one had to become an initiate to partake in that knowledge.

Seekers of this knowledge are initiated into the Mysteries through a series of symbolic rites. Then, they begin their journey towards "illumination" by being taught the symbolism of the Mysteries. Those who made it to the upper levels of the Mysteries are called Adepts and the masses of the people are referred to as the Profane.

There are usually three degrees of initiation (this depends on the School, but is usually three). Each degree would take many years of devotion to accomplish. The symbols of the Mystery School would be taught to the initiates, but it would not be until they had reached the highest levels that they would be bestowed the True Teachings of the Mystery School. From this comes the term "Mystic," or one who is versed in the Mysteries.

Most of the great ancient philosophers were initiates of the Mystery Schools. Thus we have Pythagoras' mathematics and the Platonic Solids of Plato. These Mysteries of ancient times were actually complementary to mainstream religion. The Mystery Schools taught the inner symbolic meanings of the gods that the masses worshiped.

The Mystery Schools existed worldwide, The Brahman School of India; to the Egyptian Mysteries, to the Chaldeans, the Greeks, Eleusinians, the Eastern Schools, the Babylonians, and so on. The Mystery System even existed in the cultures of the Amerindians (Mayans, Hopi, Inca, Navajo, etc.). In fact, even Christianity began as a Mystery School with the Gnostics. Though there are many Mystery Schools all over the world, their teachings are fundamentally the same.

The religion of the Mystery Schools is astrotheology and the worship of the Natural. The main object of their worship was the Sun, the Light of the World, and the Giver of Life.

The unfathomable state of existence is called the Absolute, or "God". The Sun is considered an emblem of God's love, in that all life on Earth depended upon the Sun. The Sun, often referred to as "the Risen Savior", rose every morning and vanquished the cold and the darkness.

The most important thing to the Mystery Schools is symbolism. The Symbol is a powerful force. Everything we know is in terms of symbols. For example, words and language are all symbols. The Mystery Schools held symbolism to be the best way to convey their knowledge. Contained within a seemingly simple icon is an immense amount of meaning which only the initiated would have knowledge of because they are taught.

The Mayan Calendar is a teaching of Creation. It is a time line for the entire Cosmos and the True purpose of human history. The Maya conceive the Universe as being created approximately sixteen billion years ago. The creation didn't happen all at once. Their Calendar gives the dates of nine steps of Creation that will have occurred from the beginning until the Calendar ended December 2012 – From the 12th Insight by James Redfield. There is great Mystery in the Calendar. Until recently science had no understanding - then science made similar discoveries and confirmed the "Big Bang" and an ever expanding Universe.

Look at the Mayan and Egyptian pyramids and hieroglyphics – All pictures and symbols that tell their story and Truth. A Mystery to most – this is why the Mystery Schools - To educate and To Perpetuate the Knowledge.

Working with these Skulls over the last two plus years has been like attending a mystery school, with new information, meaning and knowledge coming forth.

This is the purpose and function of the Crystal Skulls – Permanent data bases of information found nowhere else. The Original 13 Crystal Skulls are Libraries of knowledge that are Magical, Mystical and Mysterious.

The Information about Mystery Schools is important as related to the Mayans for the Truth of their culture has been a Mystery. The TRUTH of the Mayans is being released by the Elders to help guide Humanity during the Earth Changes.

There 52 Crystal Skulls are according to the knowledge and wisdom of the Elders as presented by Carlos Barrios– one for each year on the Medicine Wheel.

Thirteen years per season:
Spring ages 1 to 13 years – 13 the year of Initiation.
Summer is 13 to 26 years.
Autumn is 26 to 39 years and
Winter 39 to 52 year

After 52 years one is honored and starts over at a higher level of experience, knowledge and wisdom. That's why Grandparents and young children get along; they are in the same place on the Medicine Wheel.

We continue with the Teachings of Skull 6.

March 17, 2011 – Shamanic Journeys to Skull 6:

Questions Asked:

Please show us the Energy of Skull 6
Please show us the information of Skull 6
Does the Skull have Sounds? If so, what are they and why are they important?

SOUND:

The Sound of Skull 6 is the sound of laughter, happiness and joy of Lovers and children. It is the birds singing, the cicadas chirping with the sounds of frogs and crickets. It is the gentle breeze rustling through the leaves of the trees. All of the sounds of Skull 6 are warm fuzzy sounds of feel good vibrations, raising the energy of all those around listening.

ENERGY:

The Energy of Skull 6 is the shining golden rainbow of Light – shot through with the Divine Feminine Pink for Serenity, Green for Peace and Mother of Pearl for Love and Wisdom and with the Divine Masculine of Turquoise Blue for Communication, Indigo Blue for Insight and Visions and Purple for Divine Connection.

The Energy of Skull 6 is:
- It is swirling, connecting Heaven and Earth.
- It is the warrior who is charged with keeping the Peace, the Balance.
- It is the golden Summer Sun
- It is the Mother keeping the Peace in her family and in the community

As Skull 6 am a circle around the Star swirling the gold of the Christ Consciousness with the other colors mingling in a swirling rainbow.

I radiate the Balance of the Masculine and Feminine
I radiate as if they are a six pointed Star and I am the 7th point, the circle/Skull

The Mother holds the Energy for all in her grounded beingness – giving birth to the daughter of Love and Peace whose Holy Soul brings Serenity. That is the way of the Feminine and the continuation of All That Is.

The Masculine brings the Heaven's "Spark of Life" – The God Connection to the Mother. She brings him a Son who's Spirit has the ability to communicate Knowledge and Insight with the Daughter and Family. The six pointed star is the family created by Lovers – creating Abundance of Balance with the Holy Spirit and Holy Soul – Dancing with the Mother and Father, Son and Daughter.

The Abundance of the Soul and Spirit pour forth with faith, happiness, hope, charity and Love.

The Six Pointed Star:

The Upper Point represents Father – Spiritual Body (M) with the points on either side representing the Feminine with the Etheric Body = Pink and Green = Astral Body (F) Pink and Green are the colors of the heart chakra and LOVE

97

The next two points are Masculine Energy of Emotional Body = Turquoise and Indigo = Mental Body

The Bottom Point is Mother = Physical Body, the Feminine

The message of Skull 6 is Balance of the masculine and feminine – embodying our Divinity.

The Time is NOW!

CRYSTAL SKULLS, LOVE, PASSION AND PURPOSE
By: Gina O'Connor – USA and Holland

My love of crystal skulls began a few years ago in conjunction with a spiritual retreat I organized in Sedona, Arizona to explore Energy Consciousness. Initially, the retreat did not include crystal skulls, but the skulls happened make themselves known during this retreat on several occasions. I have to thank, Gary, the manager of the center, who first introduced me to two of his crystal skulls when I went to visit the retreat center prior to the event.

Before that time, I had almost no knowledge of crystal skulls. He was excited to show me two of his skulls so I could feel their wonderful energies. The first skull was made of clear quartz. Holding that skull, I felt an intense beam of white light enter my system.

The second skull he handed me was made of shimmering blue pietersite. Immediately it felt as if my hand chakras were opening wider and wider and energy flowed back and forth between me and the skull. I began also to have visions by looking into the skull's shining depths. I saw native peoples who had once lived in the area on that land in the past. I saw many things and was taken on a journey that could have gone on and on. My heart opened to the skull so that I felt very attached and yearned to stay with it and the energies. I really did not want to let it go, but I had to of course hand it back. Gary explained that I had helped to open the skull and activate it for new work and healing. He began to feel his skull in an entirely new way. It made me feel good to know that I could help Gary and the skull in some way to work together on a deeper level. And I was also grateful for what the skull gave to me. To this day, I reminisce about that skull. On some level, we are still connected. I am also grateful to Gary for that life-changing moment.

During the week of the retreat in Sedona, I had the extra-ordinary opportunity to meditate with a very large group of crystal skulls. Each one felt completely different and gave me a different story and energy. Some made me laugh with joy. Other skulls made me feel as if I was experiencing different life-times and dimensions. In particular, a large kambaba skull really made an impression on me; I felt my auric field extending into chakras which exist high above my crown. This skull also showed me a beautiful star being whom I felt related to. After that time, I was deeply fascinated with crystal skulls. I felt a very deep connection that I cannot totally explain, but felt very natural to me.

From then on, almost all my spiritual retreats include crystal skulls. I have organized retreats with crystal skulls in Mallorca, England, Holland, Cornwall, Ireland, Greece, USA, and Mexico. When I am not organizing retreats, I still take them everywhere I go, particularly to sacred sites. I feel this is important for a variety of energetic healing reasons – for individual healings and also for the land. Some of the reasons I am aware of ahead of time and other reasons are often revealed to me later. The skulls assist in raising the vibrations, frequencies and light wherever I share them globally. They help in speeding up processes of spiritual development and transformation. For many people, the skulls clear paths and point out opportunities and insights through synchronicities. They can help because they often mirror and uncover aspects of our highest selves. If one is ready to embrace transformation, then the skulls provide a lot of support and love. They are helpful in many individual ways, to many different people.

Always, I knew my purpose with the skulls is to help others. I work with crystal skulls in a variety of ways to do this. One specialty I have is sharing insights I receive while meditating with them. I experience so much wisdom, inspiration, and energy through this process. The skulls provide special communication with amazing insights and guidance. I could not have imagined the many kinds of information that could come through including: quantum-physics, chemistry, angels, stars and constellations, beings from other dimensions, time, space, inter-dimensional travel, and so much more. When asked, they answer questions for people and me, often through songs, poetry, words, images, feelings, and even holograms.

Their answers are often humorous, yet very profoundly layered with words and symbols meaning more than one thing at time. I also work with the skulls during energy healing sessions. They are able to get at the root causes, speeding the healings, on the DNA level. Besides that, I work with them in Inca shamanism, Oneness/Deeksha, journeying and sacred sounds.

Also, I provide homes and connections for crystal skulls. I feel I am a bridge to bring understanding, oneness, and healing as an ambassador for them. The crystal skulls have brought much transformation and healing also in my own life as well as passion and purpose. The synchronicities and magical experiences are endless! They even led me to my soul partner and love, moving me across the globe from the US to Holland, where we now reside.

What else can the crystal skulls do? They are helpful in so many ways! One thing I have noticed is that they are very loyal and protective -especially the ancient Mongolian ones I care take, but also the other ones. Here are a couple of examples. One night I was sleeping and awakened by my dogs barking loudly at my former home. I felt a sense of unease like something was outside in the yard. Right then, I felt that the skulls were circling and putting up a protection all around my yard, like guards in an army. Immediately I felt protected and comforted and safe.

A similar event happened another night. A strong tornado with lightning bolts came in the night. I was awakened abruptly by this flash of lightning illuminating my bedroom. In that moment, I "saw" all my crystal skulls on my bed with me..! Yet, they were actually downstairs in a grid. This led me to feel and understand their protective function and desire to help me always.

Since my first experiences with them, I've known they were there to help me to help others and vice versa. My mission with the crystal skulls corresponds to my overall purpose in this lifetime to provide assistance for planetary and interplanetary healing, understanding, and creative expression in these times. It may also be that is a continued mission which is also taking place in and through other dimensional fields beyond time and space, and other lifetimes, along with other parts of my soul family, interplanetary beings, guides, and angels, and highest self. Additionally, I greatly enjoy and feel connected to the mineral and crystal realms that I have been working with in this lifetime since childhood. The journey with the crystal skulls (and the crystals) has given me much joy and feeling of adventure, happiness, and way of residing in, activating, and experiencing light, love, heart centeredness, self-empowerment, healing, and high levels of conscious being.

My relationship with the crystal skulls is a two-way street, as any balanced relationship should be. If you ask me do I own a crystal skull, I will say, "No." I am their "care-taker" for a time. The term, "owning" implies that they are objects devoid of spirit. Since I feel their energies as spirits, master, angels, star beings and soul groups, I prefer to say I care take the skull for a while, but actually I think they take care of me as well. It is a mutual relationship of love and respect. I love their energies and see something special in each carving, stone, and the spirit within it. I love to experience and surround myself with their manifesting energies. And I also want to share these variations with others around the world. By care-taking this group energy, I hope to give something special to the world and people- something to experience, find healing, insight, awareness, education, and joyfulness in. It is also not unusual for people who get into crystals skulls to find that they grow a large family. It may be that the skulls like the group energy. I think that's true. They really are all about Oneness and Unity within Diversity.

Do I recommend working with crystal skulls? Yes, I do. However, I do not feel it is necessary to convert anyone to any spiritual belief or practice. It is up to each person to choose that for him/herself and see what resonates best. If a person is drawn to crystal skulls, then I do advocate spending some time experiencing them in her/his own way with an open heart and positive mindset. They can enhance any spiritual practice and bring a lot of love, support, and healing to one's life. They certainly have been a blessing in my life.

Love and Light,
Gina O'Connor
http://www.internationalspiritualexperience.com or
http://www.facebook.com/Ise.org

CRYSTAL SKULL 7

AKASHIC RECORDS QUESTIONS:

What Say You regarding Skull 7?
What additional information do we need regarding Skull 7?

Look up healing modality called Soul Retrieval that you learned in 1997 – find notes and get book. Go to the end of this chapter for this information under the Shamanic Journeys Section for Skull 7.

What is the significance of number 21?

It is as Marlene said it is 7x3 = 21. It is the number 3 spot on the Medicine Wheel. Twenty One (21) relates to emotions. More research needed on numbers 2 and 1.

The number one is the center, the point, the "seed" within all things. It is the circle, the circumference, embracing all things in evolution.

Every number divided by itself remains one and one multiplied by itself remains one.

The One is a simple Spiritual principle for a Supreme Being/Force called by a 1,000 names:

One = Creator, "*let there be Light*"

10/1 = Shaman brings One into vibratory sound

19/10/1 = the One movement of living truth that passes through all obstacles, the cycle of sacrifice. 19 is the "living truth" by maintaining contact with creative spirit and the soul of nature, staying centered while finding the way.

28/10/1 = the One of wisdom that rests in repose, embracing the Light of the Creator, the Sound of the Shaman and the movement within. This implies transcendence of the first seven worlds and of the seven deadly sins.

Two expresses a polarity and the nature of substance and matter.
Two is the first even number.
Two is the "Mother" number.
Two overlapping circles become two producing the vesica pisces, giving birth to all things in sacrifice like a mother.
Two creates a wave and from the wave comes the sea of vibrations.
Two = Primal Waters – the sea of subtle energy as the primal substance.

11/2 = subtle energy and matter.
20/2 = the circulation of these vibrations wedded to the Light.
29/11/2 = subtle energy vibrationally becomes pure harmonics.

This Research on 2 and 1 is from the Numerology Books *"Destiny"* by Rowena P. Kryder and *"Numerology Made Easy"* by W. Mykian.

Seven represents a wholeness of vibratory powers through the addition of the four elements to the three powers/principles.

7 is the number of days in the week
7 is the number of days in each phase of the Moon Cycle,
7 control the Waters in the West position on the Medicine Wheel.
7 is the number of chakras/Energy points in the human body
7 Colors of the rainbow
7 Colors of the human energy systems called chakras
7 Visible Planets in our Solar System
7 activates and animates all things

Skull 7 is the Healer's Skull. It is in the West on the Medicine Wheel.

The Divine Feminine of Skull 7 is imbued with all of the attributes before it:

$1 + 2 + 3 = 6 + 1 = 7;$
$2 + 5 = 7$ and
$3 + 4 = 7$

Seven is immutable – One of the most powerful numbers on the Medicine Wheel for it is the culmination of the five Elements plus the Balance of Six plus the One that brings healing on an Emotional Level.

The West on the Medicine Wheel and in Pagan Tradition is Water, the Element of Emotion. Therefore Skull 7 is for the Healing of Emotions. It is supported by the Eight of the North, the Earth – the place of Spiritual

Healing, but first we must acknowledge how battered most Beings, especially Humans, become from neglect of their Emotional Self.

This is the place of Soul Retrieval and where Shamanic Healing occurs. The Healing of Family wounds can also occur with the Akashic Records combined with Reiki and Dar'Shem.

Emotional wounds can also be cleared with the scent of Therapeutic Grade Essential Oils that cross the blood/brain barrier going straight to the Limbic System of the Brain where trauma is stored.

(I continue to use all of these modalities, my favorite is Shamanic Healing and I use Young Living Therapeutic Grade Essential Oils on daily basis, whether to anoint or ingest.)

Skull 7 is the Seventh Chakra at the top of the human skull – this is where Energy Healing begins in our bodies with activation of our generating crystal – our Pineal Gland.

The 7th Chakra is the Exit and Entry point for all Shamanic Journeys; it is the Shaman's Chakra.

The 7th Chakra is the Point of Receiving information from the Universe/Creator/God, the downward flow of Quantum Healing of non-locality.

Skull 7 has all of the information necessary for healing emotional wounds at the Quantum Level. This healing of ourselves includes the immediate family as well as the Ancestors and Decedents.

Skull 7 represents that place where Love of the Earth, the Feminine is necessary.

Love Heals All and the Earth is the Source of Love; The Mothers Love for All of Her Children.

Skull 7 is where the Mothering Gene in the DNA occurs. It is the next logical step after 6 – the Lovers. Children, whole and pure are entering the World through the Waters of the Womb, the very same Water as the Oceans, the birth place of Life on Earth. At birth most adults in Western culture are wounded children of wounded children.

Skull 7 sits in the place we learn to help the children maintain their purity and Wholeness. That is the purpose of the "Indigo and Crystal Kids." Marilee and Marlene are Indigos that are 25 years ahead of the wave, to pave the way – Way Showers, along with many other Light Bearers that came through after World War II. James Twyman calls this group the *"Golden Indigos."*

There is extreme Emotional Woundedness that comes from the War on Humanity and the Planet by greedy corporations, dictators and the extreme religions as well as the political extremes on both the left and right, the Republicans and Democrats in the United States.

The left dis-empowers with handouts causing generations on "The Dole."

The right dis-empowers by taking away individual rights and lower wages – taking jobs elsewhere.

The war machine is very dis-empowering as it takes valuable resources from the budget that be spent elsewhere for the "greater good of humanity". This is true for almost every country with a military force.

Because of the Bible's Book of Revelation and the Mayan Calendar end date of December 21, 2012, factions in both the Muslim faith and within the Judeo-Christian beliefs say that the destruction of the Earth/Armageddon will bring forth the return of either the 12th Imam or the 2nd Messiah.

In both cases it is believed that the "True Believers" will be protected and saved.

This is not the case – The Twelfth Imam and the Messiah are returning through each individual consciousness.

My personal experience is that Each One of us is Embodying Our Unique Divinity ... Bringing Heaven on Earth. This is our Soul's growth.

Skull 7 has Emotional Wholeness and Purity.

Skull 7 allows that consciousness to enter the physical temple of the Human Body through the Crown of Chakra 7.

Skull 7 is the Consciousness that loves so deeply that it cares for the trees and plants; the insects, the birds, the fish and animals.

Skull 7, in the West, is the place of Emotional Healing on the Medicine Wheel. Skull 7 comes with Pure Love. This is the place of children coming forth from the Waters. Just as all life on Earth came forth from the Waters – The Waters of Life, the seas and oceans.

SHAMANIC JOURNEYS to Skull 7:

What is the Sound of Skull 7?
Please Show us the Energy of Skull 7
Please show us the information of Skull 7

The Akashic Records and the Shamanic Journeys together create a wholeness of Information. This is very important at this time where all emotions are highly exaggerated. Maintaining your higher awareness of Oneness is critical at this time.

SOUND of Skull 7:

The Sound of Skull 7 is the sound of the Crystal Bowls, Prayers, Chanting, the steady Drum beat, the flowing waters, the Didgeridoo, Tingsha, Tibetan Bowls, Flutes and Rattles. The Sounds of Skull 7 are the sounds of all Indigenous Cultures Worldwide.

ENERGY of Skull 7:

The Energy of Skull 7 is a circle of wholeness. Skull 7 is about the higher finer vibrations of Love that bring wholeness – A swirling Spiral of green and pink with touches of purple and white. Swirling up to the heavens and back down through the Chakras of Humans and the Chakras of the Earth into the crystalline core.

Skull 7 is all about healing the wounds that benign neglect causes as well as the wounds caused by overt neglect and abuse, physical, mental, emotional and spiritual. It is about paying attention to our feelings about ourselves so we can heal our relationships – beginning by remembering SELF LOVE. The Love we were born with – The Love for All of Creation. Remembering we are a part of The One/the Creator/ Source.

As we remember how to shine our Lighted Love for ourselves, we begin healing our own wounds.

As we remember to be grateful, appreciate and Love All the Souls who lowered their own Lighted Love to teach the lessons and provide growth born of chaos, fear, victimization. These wonderful courageous Souls give us the individual lessons required for us to return to Wholeness.

Addiction of any kind is an Emotional Wound begging for Unconditional Love and Acceptance. It requires a safe haven in the midst of chaos. The Western Culture, especially in the United States, is a very wounding addictive culture. Media of all kinds continually bangs the drum for more, more and more of the "latest greatest." When we don't have it, can't afford it or can't compete we adopt aberrant behavior of greed, deceit and addiction. When we become addicted, whether it is to shopping, sex, work, money, collecting stuff, drugs, alcohol, sugar and eating is Self-Abuse. We are calling in all of the lower vibration emotions of anger, anxiety, aggression, sadness/grief, carelessness, confusion, delusion, depression, fear, greed, hesitation, lust, power, projection, rationalization and worry.

The effects of these feelings and emotions are:

Anger affects the Liver
Grief and Sadness affect the Lungs
Stress affects the Heart and Brain
Fear affects the Kidneys causing Kidney failure.

Release these 7 destructive emotions and you can be well by staying happy, feeling good, looking good and doing good.

All of these lower vibrations deny the wholeness and purity each person was born with and creates a cycle of Self Abuse. It can also begin with unrequited love, abandonment or rejection in early childhood. Soul Retrieval is particularly successful in restoring the high finer vibrations and attributes of Love to the body and healing specific childhood traumas.

According to Aeoliah – "Self Abuse is often unconscious with complete lack of awareness. Taking responsibility for the cause, whether from this life time or from all of the past lifetimes, when we had our first experience of separation, duality, conflict and pain. Self-Abuse is a form of self – punishment and can be Karmic payback from other lifetimes in which we all participated in as human beings. We choose people in our lives to act out a form of self-punishment because we haven't forgiven or released our own guilt or self-judgment for an experience when we were the abuser or "villain" in another lifetime.

107

The Quantum Healing starts the moment we take responsibility for the cause of our "wrong thinking" perpetrated by our culture where denial, repression, and guilt all contribute to what is called "normal, healthy society." By letting go of our "Stinking Thinking," as AA calls it, then healing can begin. The healing can be miraculous and in some cases instantaneous.

Skull 7 teaches Quantum Healing of forgiveness, non-judgment and releasing guilt and control to have "good thinking" in alignment with all of the attributes of Love. When we recognize that every act is an act of Love then a Healing and Teaching occurs. The first step is taking responsibility for our thoughts.

Skull 7 will show us how to heal and function to the beat of our own drum – our own Heartbeat. The Healing comes from listening to our own Heart and honoring the messages that only come in silence or on a sound wave of the Crystal Bowls and Drums. The "Ah Ha" moment of awareness and recognition allows space for action to be taken to change, causing a Healing within the Heart.

When we change our "wrong thinking" about our situation and what is going on inside us and in our World – We Change. We raise our Vibration towards Unconditional Love and Acceptance. Each time we do this we raise our vibration thus raising the vibrations all around us. As we keep raising our vibrations there is a cleaning, a clearing out and a restoration of the DNA towards wholeness.

Living as if you are a part of Nature, of All that is, will accelerate the Restoration with more "Ah Ha" moments found only in aloneness and organized Vision Quests of the Native American cultures. They originally lived in Harmony with the land and the entire natural World including all plants, animals, birds, insects, microorganisms, crystals and rocks, as part of One giant Community provided by Great Spirit or Creator.

Thus the Sound of Skull 7 is the Sound of the Drum, the flowing Waters, the Didgeridoo, the Tingsha, Tibetan Bowls, Rattles, Flutes and Crystal Bowls – The sounds of all indigenous cultures.

In Aeoliah's book, "AWAKENING Your Inner Light, Healing Self – Abuse and Reclaiming Your True Identity," he claims that there is a Seven (7) Step Recovery Program for Healing Emotional Abuse. Seven Steps correspond to Skull 7.

The Seven Step Recovery Program:

Acknowledge the Emotion
Do Not Judge Yourself or the Emotion
Validate Yourself
Re-parenting: Nurturing and Mothering you inner Child
Forgiveness
Transmutation
Acceptance and Integration

These steps take stamina, perseverance, courage and continual adjustment – the ebb and flow of the waves of the ocean.

For me, when I was home healing my cancer naturally, forgiveness was the most effective tool to clear the anger in my liver. Cancer was in my liver, my right lung and right breast caused my aberrant thinking and the massive amounts radiation that I received just prior to my Near Death Experience. I was injected with nuclear medicine and an x-ray was taken one inch at a time to see what a body full of blood clots does to the cardio-vascular system and the lungs. There was much trauma and the experience of pure Love and Compassion of the NDE.

I'd like to share my personal forgiveness prayer with you. It was my mantra all day and night. Now I use it at least once a day and have discovered that addressing individual organs and joints receive forgiveness and feel better. Try it!

My Personal Forgiveness Prayer:

I forgive myself for all of my Errors.
I forgive Everyone and Everything that has hurt me knowingly and unknowingly.
I ask forgiveness for myself from anyone or anything that I may have hurt, knowingly or unknowingly.
I do this forgiveness work for my past, for the present through All Time and Space with Gratitude for my Healing.

Say this Prayer in rounds of four; four times each – one each for the Spirit, The Emotions, The Mind and The Body. Please use this prayer whenever you feel the need.

Prayer is another form of Quantum Healing as defined earlier. When we pray with gratitude and appreciation as if it has already happen we create change to a higher vibration. There is no specific local – it is everywhere, in the ethers.

This forgiveness Prayer is similar to the Hawaiian technique used by their Kahunas and Medicine People called: Ho'oponopono Ho' oponopono.

Ho'oponopono means I love you, I'm sorry, please forgive me, and thank you or
I'm sorry; please forgive me, I Love You (*I add with gratitude – I also use this prayer on my lungs, my heart, my liver as well as my brain and whole body and when any one, especially certain family members upset me with their "stinking thinking and behavior."*

In Hawaii (using only this Prayer with the prisoner's file and no personal contact) Dr. Len, a mental health professional, emptied the prison for the criminally insane, one person at a time. This is the Power of Prayer, of Quantum Healing.

Ho'oponopono (Ho oponopono, Hooponopono) is a means for being aligned with existence, All That Is. Most important of all, ho'oponopono (ho oponopono, hooponopono) is a big help in clearing you out to make room for your healing to occur. Healing and wellbeing is an "Inside Job".

It Is All About You:

The key aspect of ho'oponopono is this: everything comes from you. This is referred to as 100 percent responsibility. It means that every problem you experience is happening because of you. In ho'oponopono the problem is never with someone else – it's in you.

Responsibility of ho'oponopono:

Can a person not accept 100 percent responsibility and still practice the ho'oponopono method? Yes. But the belief here is that seeing circumstances as being caused by external events, while at the same trying to use ho'oponopono, is neutralizing the method's effects.

Responsibility is the key to how ho'oponopono works. Responsibility does not mean you need to blame yourself for problems – just know that problems you experience are there for you to resolve and learn from. Taking Responsibility is a gift you give yourSelf.

Getting to the issue:

Ho'oponopono practice is not difficult, though it takes discipline. The results from using ho'oponopono on a consistent basis can be incredible. How to use ho'oponopono? Say the Prayer in rounds of four – four times each round for the body, mind, emotions and spirit.

Say the Prayer 'I love you, I'm sorry, please forgive me, thank you.'

The key to the ho'oponopono process is consistent application. The more you put ho'oponopono to use, the more you can experience life changing results.

This information is from the website: http://www.hooponoponohelp.com/

Healing Prayer – Church of the Divine Mother:

Another Healing Prayer that was written by Marlene and Marilee with two other Ministers for the Church of the Divine Mother. It is from the Akashic Records of Priestess Juanita E. Miller; Bishop Mary E. Perez; Priestess Marlene K. Rhodes; Bishop Marilee A. Snyder-Nieciak. This was truly a group process and everyone contributed a portion and it took four months to write meeting two times per month.

The prayer is called "Church of the Divine Mother Liturgical Healing Prayer." It can be found below and in our next book – "Ancient Wisdom for Now; the Trilogy, Book II, Prayers and Meditation."

When this Prayer is said out Loud to the Person in need you can actually feel the Healing Energy of the Prayer descend from the Heavens.

It is best to say the Prayer in rounds of three minimally for the Body, Mind and Spirit.

This Prayer can be used for countries at war, for pets, for groups and for individual families and individuals. Marlene and I often used this prayer before beginning our sessions with the Skulls. We asked for healing for ourselves and our families.

Church of the Divine Mother Liturgical Healing Prayer:

We welcome and Honor the Spirits of the four Elements,
Earth, Air, Fire and Water,
We welcome and Honor God, Goddess and Holy Spirit to
Create the Divine Trinity for Balance.
We come in Love calling on Father God
Acknowledging the Healing Powers of the
Forces of Light for the Highest and Best Good of ALL.
We Honor each Being and
Honor the Healing that has occurred; is occurring and that will continue to occur
With Deep Appreciation.
Divine Mother of ALL, We lift our Hearts to You.
Fill us with Your Essence that our Oneness is Complete in All You have created.
Mother, Father God, Beloved Creator,
You have created us in the image of Your Perfection.
Guide us now as we seek to Assist
_____ (Individual Name; Family Name; Group Name)
To uplift their Vibration so that they are in Harmony with the Perfection of ALL That Is.
We Give Thanks for This Healing.
Thy Will Be Done, On Earth as it is in Heaven
Amen and So It Is

Once we have prayed, we then, in the order of things, take responsibility for own health and wellbeing. We seek and find alternative health care practitioners using Ancient Healing Techniques that we resonate with such as therapeutic grade Essential Oils, Massage Therapy, Reiki and Dar'Shem, Reflexology, Energy Workers of various modalities, Medicine People and Shamans.

Soul Retrieval:

"It is time for all to collect back our lost pieces and remember why we are born into this world. Then, we are truly healed and can live our lives in harmony and help others do the same." From the back cover of Soul Retrieval, Mending the Fragmented Soul by Sandra Ingerman.

This seems to be the perfect place to discuss Soul Retrieval as it is an Ancient Shamanic Healing Technique requiring excellent "journeying" skills to bring energy back to the client, whether human or animal. This work is the work of the Shaman. *(It is my favorite because everyone is so different.)*

Skull 7, at the very beginning of this chapter through the Akashic Records suggested that I find my Soul Retrieval notes and book.

Today is April 6, 2011 and I found all 38 pages of my notes and a Monthly Aspectarian article called "Shamanism and Soul Retrieval" written by my friend, colleague and shaman, Paula Rosenfeld, dated April 1997.

In late August of 1997, I studied Soul Retrieval with Sandra Ingerman, the foremost authority and author of the book "Soul Retrieval". The five day residential class was held at Brietenbush Springs, Oregon and sponsored by the Foundation for Shamanic Studies.

Skull 7 is the Skull of the Healer, the Shaman, Medicine Person and Quantum Healing.

One of the healing techniques of the Shaman is Soul Retrieval, Mending the Fragmented Self, another form of Spiritual Healing where the spiritual wounds manifest illness physically and emotionally.

It is my personal belief system that all physical disease is the result of spiritual and emotional wounds.

For me it is an extraordinary experience of remembering. I have had approximately 35 Soul Retrievals from various Shamanic Practitioners to help me heal my wounds from my family and from my lives. The primary Soul Retrieval Practitioner is Paula Rosenfeld, who I met through a 1995 Akashic Records Reading by Linda Howe, who performed my first and second Soul Retrievals in 1992 and 1993. Linda was one of my teachers from January of 1991 to January of 2000 and I am grateful.

At some level, we are all wounded children of wounded children back down the family linage. Our wounds begin between 0 and 5 years of age. As we heal ourselves and our Soul, we heal our ancestors and our children. If we go back one generation, then we heal all the way back and into the future.

In our era of continual bombardment of violence in the media, we hurt spiritually, emotionally, mentally and physically. We need to heal more than our physical body, which can be hurt and traumatized, including with certain medical procedures, especially invasive surgical procedures. Soul Retrieval restores the fragmented bits of our Soul (that left to live in our electromagnetic field) to their rightful place in our physical body. It is a very powerful technique that restores "the Universal Life Force Energy" to the Being. Restoring Power means restoring the ability to use Energy.

The Foundation for Shamanic Studies was founded by Michael Harner. In teaching Cross-Cultural Shamanism, FSS talks about three major Causes of Illness, which is usually a combination of the three.

Power = Energy by Shamanic definition so we are talking about the loss of energy. The three major causes are:

*Loss of Power: Chronic problems, colds, flu, chronic depression, suicidal thoughts are examples of Power Loss. The most common sign of Power Loss is Chronic Misfortune. Something is missing – The Shaman brings back the "Power" in the form of a protective animal.

*Spiritual Intrusion: When there is no power, there is a loss. The Universe can't stand a void, which is then filled with a Spiritual Intrusion. Spiritual Intrusion manifests as localized pain or intrusion like Lung Cancer or Stomach Cancer. It is misplaced Energy that needs to be returned to its home. Shamans pull out or suck out the intrusion and transmute the energy to healing energy.

Dr. Amit Goswami talked about "bad thinking" that needed to be changed for a quantum healing. Spiritual Intrusion comes from negative thought forms. We need to learn the difference between expressing and sending out anger. People can create their own Intrusion when they can't express their anger.

Epidemics come from many people expressing their Emotions – Think about that and the power of feeling thought. Quantum Healing is reversing those thoughts.

*Soul Loss: The third cause of illness is Loss of Soul – Soul is our Life Force, our Essences. When we experience any emotional or physical trauma, we dissociate. In Shamanism, a part of our Life Force goes away waiting where we do not have access to its Essences. Someone has to go get that Essence and bring it back.

114

Some of the causes of "Soul Loss" are:

Post-traumatic Stress Syndrome
- Surgery
- War Time
- Experience Violence
- Natural Disasters – Look at Japan's disasters
- Addiction – cause and symptom
- Abuse
- Divorce
- Physical Trauma
- Alarm Clocks and Phones
- Chronic Fatigue

Death is a cause because people, who can't get over the death or loss of a loved one, may experience Soul Loss.

People who feel separated from other people including their families and feel that they cannot connect with other people have experienced Soul Loss.

The role of the Shaman is to retrieve the Soul. In old cultures, the Soul was never gone for more than three days. Now, when we go back, we go back years, looking for the first Soul part that is lost. It has been scientifically proven that our behavior is completely formed between ages zero and five years. Shamans deal with feelings and emotions so the client can change their thinking.

We constantly hurt people with our words and we are constantly hurt by other people's words and actions towards us.

Sometimes a Soul won't come back when there is Soul Loss because someone stole it. Incest survivors talk about their Soul leaving their body or having it taken. People steal a Soul Essences out of jealousy; for example, a depressed parent wants the Light of a new child.

In our culture, stealing Soul Essences isn't done intentionally. It is passed down. It is not even conscious.

Co-dependency – both people stealing each other's Soul and they become very much enmeshed. We see this in alcoholic families. When someone is dying and they don't want to – they will steal Soul Essences.

Yet the Truth is: No One Can Use another Person's Light or Power. That is a Lose/Lose Situation. The Thief is burdened with unusable Energy and the victim is left with less Power. Most thieves feel that their survival depends on holding on to the Soul Essences. With Chronic Fatigue clients, the return of their Soul Essences actually changes their blood test results.

As in all Quantum Healing, there is always a surprise element – We look for the surprise and share it a kind and loving way.

Pure Essences that have no fear have returned to you giving additional strength, hope, love… whatever the Shaman was told about the Surprise Essences that returned. Very little conversation is needed as words take away the Power of the healing process. The client needs to experience the Victory, the Accomplishment.

Soul Retrieval is truly a Celebration towards well-being. Shamanism; Indigenous Healing and Quantum Healing are very results oriented.

Coma is Soul Loss and is very difficult to work with because of Life Support.

We say "Welcome Home" both after the actual Soul Retrieval and as the ending to the session with Thanks and Gratitude. Our work for today is finished.

The Soul Retrieval is the beginning of the work if the client chooses to continue.

When working with the Power of the Universe there is tremendous Healing and Energy. This is the Magic of Quantum Healing in its many forms.
My third book in this Trilogy is *"Ancient Wisdom for NOW! Natural Healing with Shamanism and Creator's Gift Pure Essential Oils"*.

As stated on the first page, *"Shamanism is the cutting edge of 40,000 year old Technology."* In book III, we will go into greater depth with many Soul Retrieval case studies. There will also be case studies from other modalities that both my clients and I have personally experienced.

Skull 7 shares in some way all Natural Healing...

CRYSTAL SKULL 8

It is March 28, 2011; we work with Skull 8 = 3 + 28 + 2011 = 31 + 4 = 35/8. An 8 day for Skull 8

AKASHIC RECORD QUESTIONS and ANSWERS:

What say you regarding Skull 8?
What additional information is there?

Marilee, dear one, 8 is your number and you know it well. Use your reference material – just as you have been doing.

- I Am Skull 8 the Earth.
- I Am Skull 8 the North on the Medicine Wheel the second time (4 x 2 = 8).
- I Am Skull 8 the Keeper of the Connection to the Heavens and to the Cosmos.
- I Am Skull 8 bringing forth Visions for a Brighter Future for All of My Children – FOR ALL OF MY CHILDREN IN A SUFFICIENT, SUSTAINABLE WAY, WITH HARMONY and BALANCE AMONG ALL ELEMENTS, ALL BEINGS and ALL INTELLIGENCES.
- I Am Skull 8 bringing forth the Creative Ideas to be discussed in the Councils of the different Nations of the Beings and Intelligences.
- I Am Skull 8 answering questions like:

What do the Trees need to be in Harmony?
What do the Insects need to be in Harmony?
What does the Soil need to be Balanced?
How do we prepare the Soil for Seed?
How can we help the Water?

- I Am Skull 8 bringing forth the Knowledge and Information. I am freely sharing it with the Circle of Elders' Council of each nation – for each species on Earth is a nation unto itself.
- I Am Skull 8 providing assistance and guidance for the selection of those Beings that can receive the Visions, Wisdom and Guidance for the Tribe.

This is the Work of the Wisdom Keepers, male and female; the Shamans, who travel the Cosmos, speaking with the Masters, Teachers and Loved Ones; The Earth Keepers, (who bring forth healing and the information provided by the Earth, The Elves and Fairies) are the perfect counter balance to the Wisdom Keepers.

AS ABOVE SO BELOW; AS BELOW SO ABOVE.

This is the flowing 8 cycles for All Species and Nations on Earth. It is important to the annual cycle of the 13 Moons and 12 Suns of the Procession of Light.

December 21, 2012 is when a new calendar count begins. So at this juncture in time the 8 is especially critical, specifically for the "Light Workers"; the Shamans; the Wisdom Keepers and the Earth Keepers. The Shift continues as an internal one for these "Way Showers" followed by others in waves. The shit will take a few years for everyone to change their thinking. Probably four years...

This is a time of Integration. A Time of Manifesting the Age of Enlightenment – The Golden Age of 1000 years of Peace on Earth

- I Am Skull 8, I Am here to assist.
- I Am Skull 8, two – 360 degree circles one on top of the other; one circle for Heaven and one for Earth; forms an 8 with constant flow of Light energy, information, guidance, healing and Love back and forth. This constant flow of energy creates and maintains the changes necessary to bring forth the Higher Vibration of the Golden Age. It requires "wake up" calls of Tornadoes, Floods, Forest Fires, Volcano Eruptions, Earth Quakes, Tsunamis, Draught and Wind Storms.

The chaos and destruction is sometimes necessary in the face of human behavior to Re-Create Heaven on Earth. Human behavior needs to change for survival of the species. The Human race needs to vertical and quantum teaching which the "wake up" will bring.

According to Rowena Pattee Kryder, Ph.D., in her book "DESTINY, Gaia Matrix Numerology," the Number 8 (Eight) has four separate stages:

*7><8 – Expansion:
The whole-heartedness of your being allows natural expansion of your essence so that you can be with all things. As you acknowledge your

mistakes and forgive yourself you will be relieved of great Soul burdens. This process enables you to expand your feelings and sense of identity.

* 7><9 – Total Presence:

The great emptiness of non-being is filled with the plenitude of presence when you are fully present without attachment. Living in the moment is living in eternity.

*35/8 – Wonder:

The resurrection of your Soul through love is opening to awe of infinite being. Your destiny involves having a child's sense of wonder while knowing the depths of the human Soul experience.

*8><9 – Return:

The purity of your being is becoming so sublime that you can now rest in non-being and return to the ultimate Source of things. Weave your path with strands of forgiveness and willingness to enter the mystery.

On Sunday April 3, after much forgiveness work on Friday, Saturday and Sunday, I actually experienced non-being at a gathering I attended where we did meditations. It was sublime. And as I was writing this I was reminded of another experience and teaching I received when the U.S. declared war on Iraq.

There was a Pipe Ceremony and we all joined in prayer at the same time. The purpose of the Pipe Ceremony was for us to ask the question "what inside of me prevents Peace."

The answer I received is:

"Judgment leads to attachment to outcome,
Attachment leads to control,
Control leads to fear
Fear is the absence of Love"

Then on the morning of September 18, 2011 as I was waking up – I saw and heard:

I release Judgment – Allowing Acceptance
I release Attachment – Allowing Truth and Trust
I release Control – Allowing the Light to Shine
I release Fear – Allowing Love to Prevail

Love is the purity of being and allows us to expand our physical being 18 inches into the Earth to receive her Love from our roots into the Root or First Chakra; to bring it up into our body and infusing our Hearts (Fourth Chakra) with Unconditional Love and carry that Love upward out of our Seventh, Eighth and Ninth Chakras into the Universe and beyond.

As we send Love upward the Universe/ the One/Creator/ Source is simultaneously sending us Light Waves that carry information, guidance and Wisdom downward, traveling the same highway in a different direction. Our challenge is to receive all of this Lighted information and Love from a place of acceptance and non-judgment so that we experience the Wonder and be in Balance and Harmony.

Skull 8 facilitates this process for the Earth and all of the inhabitants with her transmissions. The Lighted Love information dwells in all the perceived empty spaces, where in fact real communication happens on a Quantum level.

Skull 8 is everywhere, all at once, helping and guiding every Being if we but listen.

Skull 8 is about connecting the Physical World with World of Spirit and Non-locality.

Skull 8 incorporates all of the following attributes:

1. Octagon – Intermediary between the Circle of One 360 degrees and
The Square of four 90 degree angles is another 360 degrees
2. An Octave of music – the Solfaggio Scale – The Healing Sounds
3. Eight (8) is one of the Platonic solids;
4. A Hexagram used to ward off evil and evil spirits for the Pennsylvania Dutch
5. The Hexagram is the shape of the Chinese bagwa of Fung Shui for proper Energy/Chi Flow within spaces within homes or buildings and for the most beneficial placement of building on specific location.
6. The Eight directions of the Mariners Cross and Medicine Wheel.
7. The Eight directions and Seasons of the Earth/Pagan Calendar
8. Skull 8 vibrates in resonance with the ordinary human mind.

$1 + 7 = 8$
When 8 is $1 + 7$ (17) it represents the transmission of the previous seven Skulls. It is the giving birth to a new paradigm of social forms through personal empowerment and cooperation of community.

$2 + 6 = 8$

When 8 is formed by 2 + 6 of the number 26 it is also 13 x 2; the resurrection of the Soul. Like a vertical Infinity it is produced by the Expansion of the Soul as it faces the shadows. This Christ and 12 Disciples + Mary Magdalene and 12 Disciples = 13 + 13 = 26. This is the highest initiation, indicates a maturation of the Light Body through the Soul's power of Love and Forgiveness. It correlates to the keynote of "A". It sounds like "Aaaahhhh" of God, Buddha, and Allah.

$3 + 5 = 8$

When 8 is from 35 (3 +5) it is the Higher octave of Eight and the Grail Mother, the elevated mind of the Heart's intellect. 3 = masculine Triangle and 5 = feminine of the Star of Venus.

$4 + 4 = 8$

Eight as 44 is 4 + 4 = 8. This has all of the attributes of 4 squared or 2 cubed. This is a Master Number of the disciplined Disciple who is well developed physically, mentally, emotionally and spiritually. Karma re-evaluation and resurrection of finding the Wisdom and Love. The Mariner's Cross is 44.

$5 + 3 = 8$

Eight as 53 (5+3=8) is the Season of the Autumn Equinox the inner movement of healing after the autumn harvest. During Libra, Scorpio and Sagittarius is the preparation for survival of Winter and the Solstice of December. This is a courageous place. We go within to heal while balancing the act of meeting the Ancestors on All Hallows Eve and The day of the dead, depending on the culture, to honor their contributions and Transformation from form to spirit.

My birthday is September 26/8 and this information resonates deep within my Soul. As I complete this manuscript and look back over my life at age 66 moving towards 67/13/4. Amazing Changes have occurred and rapidly in the last two or three years.

Our land is called Sage Spirit Terra – Healing Spirit Land – the healing of the Soul and Spirit of all who join us in sacred ceremony on the Land.

Sage Spirit Terra's Mission is to Empower Individuals to Empower themselves and heal the planet locally.

This is all very fitting for an 8 from 26 (2 + 6). Fire and Family, Fire Transmutes and Heals the family/community.

As Above, So Below, As Below, So Above.

Friday, April 1, 2011

Shamanic Journeys to Skull 8:

What is the Energy of Skull 8?
What is the information of Skull 8?
What is the Sound of Skull 8?

I Am Sorry, Please Forgive Me, I Love You, Thank You with sincere Appreciation, I humbly ask for your information. These are the first words I heard as I journeyed to Skull 8.

SOUND:

The Sound of Skull 8 is the rustling of trees accompanied by the Lyre – God's Harp – Soothing and Gentle. The sound is the language of the Spheres, the 8 Solfaggio Tones, the Original Healing Sounds of the Universe, the Wholeness. The Solfaggio Scale is the original Healing Sounds...Deepak Chopra says that where sound is missing there is disease. The Solfaggio Tones are the Healing Sounds for the Universe.

ENERGY:

Skull 8's Energy looks like the swirling green of Earth, the blue of the oceans floating in the dark blue black purple of the Heaven with twinkling lights. Planet Earth is floating in the Universe that is a University with Halls of Records and Information being sent out as messages and prayers and opening to receive more Love and Wisdom. It is the flowing balance of masculine and feminine energy – green and red of the Earth with purple/blue and white of Spirit.

*Beautiful in its completeness is Skull 8.
*The Energy of Skull 8 is the Energy of the Master connecting Heaven and Earth.
*Two cubed 2 x 2 = 4 x 2= 8. A squared off Eight is two cubes stacked. Each square side of the cube has 360 degrees.

Skull 8 represents the effortless manifestation far beyond the Magician with his horizontal infinity sign.

122

Skull 8 is the opening to All that Is.

It Connects the Heaven's Energy, Light, Knowledge, Wisdom and Guidance deep into the Earth anchoring it 18 inches below the surface.

Skull 8 represents the 8th Chakra that is your switchboard; it expands and contracts the Energy and Information of the Earth flowing towards the Universe with Love; Information and Light Flowing towards the Earth in a never ending Continual Flow. Thus, Creating Heaven on Earth and Earth in Heaven; On Earth as it is In Heaven;

As Above So Below; As Below So Above.

Eight supports the Work of Number 7. Therefore, Skull 8 supports and completes the work of Skull 7 because:

Two expresses a polarity and the nature of substance and matter.
Two is the first even number.
Two is the "Mother" number.
Two expresses the spiritual substance of all worlds to be.
Two overlapping circles become two producing the vesica pisces, giving birth to all things in sacrifice like a mother.
Two creates a wave and from the wave comes the sea of vibrations.
Two = Primal Waters – the sea of subtle energy as the primal substance.

$11/2$ = subtle energy and matter.
$20/2$ = the circulation of these vibrations wedded to the Light.
$29/11/2$ = subtle energy vibrationally becomes pure harmonics

$2 \times 2 = 4 \times 2 = 8$
The Four is the number of purpose, completing the intention of number one and mediating the fulfillment of number 7.

$1 + 1 = 2 + 1 = 3 + 1 = 4 \times 2 = 8$ = the Octave of music, closing the scale of 7.

$1 + 7 = 8$
Skull 8 stimulates consciousness and the awareness of social harmony correlated with the sideways rotating planet Uranus which is associated with creative genius and revolutionary, sudden change.

$2 + 6 = 8$
In sacrifice, Skull 8 deals directly with the resurrection of the Soul.

123

$3 + 5 = 8$

Skull 8 from 35 is the higher octave of the Trickster and the Grail Mother, the elevated mind of the intellect.

$4 + 4 = 8$

Like a vertical Infinity sign supports. The 8 is produced from expansion of the Soul as it faces the dark nights of the Soul – The Return of the Light in Greater Brilliance, expanding the intellect with consciousness and awareness.

The circle, one or zero at the beginning has 360 degrees. The four or square has 360 degrees. This shows that attainment and fulfillment are possible here on Earth in physical body because the circle and the square both contain 360 degrees.

As an Octagon, the number 8 is the intermediary between the circle as one and the square as 4.

The simple 8 integrates experience through the mind, synchronizing the mind with changing experience.

- Skull 8 relates to Creative Genius,
- Skull 8 relates to Quick Wits
- Skull 8 relates to the ability to make precise decisions
- Skull 8 begins the first stage of Initiation – called Baptism in the Catholic Church.
- Skull 8 is symbolized by the Raven, the invisible bird that awakens consciousness as a spiritual birth. In the Pacific Northwest the Raven is the Sacred Trickster Bird insuring that his actions awaken, forcing a quick wit on all those that he plays with. The coyote is another trickster performing the same task in other geographical areas.
- Skull 8 vibrates in resonance with the ordinary human mind – the trickster.
- Skull 8 demonstrates that the Body belongs to the Earth and our Soul belongs to Source, the flow of energy.
- Skull 8 gives birth to new social forms through individual empowerment and cooperation.
- Skull 8 represents the 8 winds;
- Skull 8 represents the 8 families of the Periodic Table of Elements.
- Skull 8 represents the complete healing of the Soul of any past wounds,
- Skull 8 represents the healing of emotional conflicts in relationships,
- Skull 8 represents the Wounded Healer who evolved by forgiving all,
- Skull 8 represents the sacrifice of emotional attachments and addictions for fulfilled Aspirations in Love and business.

- Skull 8 correlates to Friday, to Venus, and the sacrament of Holy Matrimony, the marriage of body and Soul.

Once healed in seven, we move to the North to the Element of Earth, expanded energy of the Grail Mother.

The North is where we go deep within and receive the Lighted information to move forward.

- Skull 8 is about creating new visions for ourselves and the Community.
- Skull 8 supports all of the creative arts and all creative genius with us, the family groups or with the tribal groups.

Shamanic Cultures creating new things and ideas that support individual and group well-being. This is a place of growth beyond self.

Growth for the highest and best good of All. This is a place of trust where the masculine of Sky Father meets the feminine Earth Mother.

Skull 8 represents all of the 8s within the human body systems – all flowing 8 energy:

- Heart and Small Intestines – The manna of Life – receiving nourishment
- Lungs and Large Intestines – Elimination of toxicity
- Stomach and Throat – To know and speak our Truth
- Reproductive Organs and Third Eye – Centers for creativity and visions.
- Beautiful is Skull 8 in its completeness.

CRYSTAL SKULL 9

AKASHIC RECORDS:

What say you regarding Skull 9?
What additional Information is there?

Skull 9 is the completion of the Earth walk Energy. From this point on we will be working in the higher dimensions.

Skull 9 represents a completion and new beginning on the Medicine Wheel in the East for the third and last time.

This Skull is the 9th Chakra, the Energy Center of Humans and the Earth. The 8 of the Earth/ Body Energy Merges with the 8s of the Spheres. This is the place where Earth/ Body Energy Merges with Music and Light.

With the nine we walk away from the Gravity of Earth. It is Completion plus an Initiation Place. It is a place of Flight and Freedom.

Freedom is the ability to explore the Universe. It is the place where all dross is discarded so the next phase can begin.

$9 = 1 + 8$
$9 = 2 + 7$
$9 = 3 + 6$
$9 = 4 + 5$
$9 = 3 + 3 + 3$
$9 = 3 \times 3$

So each phase of the progression $1 + 2 = 3 + 3 + 3$ needs to be cleared.

The language of numbers is the language of music, computers and Light. This is the point that this language enters the Energy Field of the Human body. It is the Ninth (9th) Chakra located approximately 36 inches above the head $(3 + 6 = 9)$ and $(3 \times 6 = 36 / 9)$.

Nine times any number reduces to nine.
The nine is the language of Crystals. Skull 9 is pure white crystal.

- I Am Skull 9, the Universe's Information crossroad.
- I Am Skull 9 the Portal for Information from the Orion, Pleiades, Arcturus, Andromeda, Venus, Mercury, Mars, Uranus, Pluto, Saturn and the Great Central Sun.
- I, Skull 9 infuse the other Crystal Skulls and all of the Crystals with Universal Information.

The Pineal Gland is a crystalline structure within the human body. That is why the Seventh (7th) Chakra, the pineal gland, needs to be fully activated.
If each person's pineal is fully activated, then they can receive accurate information from Source without the barrage of media misinformation.

- I, Skull 9 bring through that which must be completed. This is the place of death – death of old ideas and ways of being.
- Skull 9 completes the cycle after Skull 8 restores the Soul.
- I, Skull 9 remove anything and everything, ideas, belief systems and beliefs that do not support the Highest Good of the Soul. The Light is so bright that it is blinding; the lower vibrations are not visible or knowable.

Skull 9 is the balance of the 6-pointed star of Skull 6 with a large equilateral triangle $= 9 = 3 + 3 + 3$. The balance is completely safe, protected and grounded on Earth.

The Language of Light also brings information to the Earth herself, so that she can make adjustments. The Earth then informs all of her children of impending change:

Which Beings and Intelligences need to transition to another plane of existence?
When is it time to move from one place to another to fulfill the Beings Purpose?
When is it time to move from Earth?

- Skull 9, as a nine, is a very high vibration with an exalted place on the Medicine Wheel.
- Skull 9 always brings new information.
- Skull 9 always means change – transition of some kind.
- Skull 9 always means completion that sometimes comes as what humans call death of the physical body.

SHAMANIC JOURNEYS: QUESTIONS for SKULL 9:

What Is the Energy of Skull 9?
What information do you wish to share with us, Skull 9?
What is the Sound of Skull 9?

SOUND:

As Skull 9, My Sound is the sound of All the Crystal Bowls and the Solfaggio Tones of the original musical scale.

ENERGY:

- I Am Skull 9, a very Bright White Light.
- I Am Skull 9, I Am Power
- I Am Skull 9, I Am Information
- I Am Skull 9, I Am Wisdom
- I Am Skull 9, I Am Guidance
- I Am Skull 9 that works with those that choose to access the higher Realms.
- I Am Skull 9 that works with those that have been doing their own healing work
- I Am Skull 9 that work with those that have steadfastly been raising their own vibration with Energy Healing, Meditation, Yoga, Akashic Records, Shamanic Journey work and Healing.
- I Am Skull 9, the Skull that holds those that are dying in my Energy. It is sometimes called the Tunnel of Light. My Energy itself is very comforting.
- I, Skull 9 Heal any residual pain from the Earth plane before the Being passes into The Light.
- I Am Skull 9 the Powerful and Compassionate Energy that is infused and filled with Unconditional Love for the completion of the Soul's Earth walk.
- I, Skull 9 Guard the Tunnel of Light with an All-Enveloping Light and Love for those that travel in their sleep and dreams to release and Heal.
- I Am Skull 9, the culmination of Human Creativity.
- I Am Skull 9, the Voice to the Upper Realms. This is the Energy I Hold!
- I Am Skull 9, the Guardian of the Gates to Heaven and to Earth. I guard the Travelers (the Shamans; the Visionaries; the Entrepreneurs; and the Light Workers).
- I Am Skull 9, the Information Highway from Heaven to Earth. All of the Angels, Archangels, Masters, Teachers and Loved Ones must pass through my portal to deliver the information.

- I Am Skull 9 the Information Highway from Earth to Heaven. I deliver your questions, your Prayers and your Healing requests from Earth to the Heavens.
- I Am Skull 9 the Condor and the Eagle, the Messengers that often pass through my portals.

The Condor and The Eagle are the only two birds that have earned the right and privilege to fly so high; taking messages and bringing back information. Use their symbols always for they, too, are protectors. When called upon they will protect you as you travel the Universe.

And You, Marilee, have always been surrounded by the Energy of the Skulls and you pass through my (Skull 9's) portals often. You have been traveling your whole life. Now you have the awareness of more than just escaping – You have the Purpose.

- I Am Skull 9 for Quantum Healing direct from Source. I Am of God. That said, Use the Skulls for Healing. The Skulls Inform with regard to Healing and often send specific healing energy to deal with specific issues.
- I, Skull 9, when integrated, make it possible to activate the Skulls within your Self.
- I Skull 9 teach that all of you deserve Abundance – in all its forms. John is a good teacher for Marilee for he shows you how to re-purpose and you Marilee are a good teacher for him for you are surrounded always by the Skulls. They have been with you since birth.
- I, Skull 9 teach You to Shine Your Light! Never lower Your Light to please others.

Skulls 10, 11 and 12 are Above corresponding with Below.

10 – Shaman Beginning
11 - Transmutation and Transformation
12 – Stability
13 – Within - Earth and the ultimate Transformation within us. Skull 13 allows us to manifest our Heart's Desires for it is Love.

The Skulls hold the Energy of God. As 13 they hold all information on Earth and beyond all the levels of the Akashic Records.

Diamond's Soul Retrieval on April 8, 2011:

Do a Soul Retrieval for Diamond, (Dog = God spelled backwards). She joins you and Marlene for the Healing Energy in the room because she knows how to receive. Per Skull 9's instructions, I did the Soul Retrieval for Diamond. These are the animals and essences that were returned to her.

Turtle:

Turtle is on her back. She now has her Home and Mother with her all the time. She now knows that she is always homing, loved and nurtured. She is Love and Loved.

Eagle:

Eagle brings her the ability to fly. She can fly to get guidance, wisdom and Light to Heal her Self and others. She will inform with Eagle.

Condor:

Condor is with Diamond now for the ability to fly and for the ability to eat her own energetic and physical carrion and dross as well as clean up after others. She will keep the spaces and Beings clean with Condor.

These animals, all three of them as a unit, bring a wholeness to her Being, as you progress, so will Diamond.

By receiving the Condor and the Eagle, Diamond integrated Skull 9 into her own Being.

RESEARCH - Gematria:

Gematria is a very ancient system of numbers encoded into sacred texts including the Bible. The Greeks, Romans, Hebrews, Egyptians, Persians and Babylonians all used Gematria in their writings – a secret code for those that had eyes to see.

Gematria codes all have one thing in common; they add up to nine; are a multiple of nine or are divisible by nine.

Gematria numbers were used by ancient peoples listed above in their systems of weights and measures.

The ancient Mayans used Gematria in their very accurate timekeeping. These people used "pi" and the "radian." As mentioned earlier the Mayans were the first to use zero (0), with a basis of 10. Skull 10 is next.

KASPER AND HIS CRYSTAL SKULL FAMILY:
By: Kirsten Hilling – Germany

My name is Kirsten Hilling I am a German Spiritual Healer, Teacher and Writer. I have the honor to care for a big crystal skull family.

At the beginning of 2010 my crystal skull Kasper informed me quite naturally that the spiritual world and the crystal skull consciousness wanted me to create a crystal skull card deck together with world-famous crystal skull experts, in order to make the messages of the crystal skulls available for the people.

I am proud to present a multitude of wonderful crystal skulls with their special energies and messages and to make people acquainted with globally working crystal skull caretakers.

It was a wonderful project of synergy and as Jaap van Etten says, "It is important because we live in a time of change, shift and transformation and the crystal skulls are the most wonderful tools to support this process."

For many years I have been passionately dedicated to the working with crystals. Thus it was not very surprising that after having worked for years with healing stones and Earthkeeper crystals, Crystal Skulls came into my life with their wonderful and powerful energy.

Since "Kasper", my first life-size smoky quartz skull, moved in, nothing has been like it was before.

Big changes and transformations have taken place and many wonderful people came into my life.

Shortly after "Kasper" arrived I had the big luck and great honor of making the acquaintance of Star Johnsen-Moser and her crystal skull Xamuku.

I had the chance to learn a lot from Star and Xamuku and I received many initiations that were important for me and my work.

The crystal skulls do not only affect my private life but are also much deployed into my work, I cannot even imagine a life before the crystal skulls from my present point of view.

Beside the crystal skulls with a human head shape I have been caretaking a crystal buffalo skull for some years now which has a direct connection to the White Buffalo Calf Woman and which facilitates our access to her.

Since Kasper was my first crystal skull coming into my life, I have a very close and deep relation to him, we communicate every day, it is like communicating with a friend, and the only difference is that we do not use spoken words to communicate, but communicate on a mental way.

Crystal skulls are tools of spiritual awareness. Within the last years I could see how a crystal skull can be a truly remarkable instrument for spiritual growth. Many researchers agree that crystal skulls do several things with energy; they can focus energy, reflect energy, refract energy, attune energy, transmit energy, transform energy, store energy and amplify energy.

People usually notice that their crystal skull is reflecting and amplifying their emotions. This is pretty challenging, because it requires self-examination, reflection and honesty. This kind of interaction makes crystal skulls a great tool for self-mastery and self-healing.

Crystal skulls are instruments of change.

Everyone who has ever worked with crystal skulls will assure you that their lives have changed a lot since they started working with crystal skulls. Life and especially a spiritual path always involve changes, without changes there can be no growth.

Apart from self-healing work, skulls can be used as a great tool in any healing session, for others as well as for animals, nature etc.

For thousands of years people have been working with crystal skulls, they are deployed in healings, rituals and ceremonies. Many indigenous people see them as "holy instruments" that will help people ascending and thus help the earth's ascension, for we can face a future full of peace, harmony and love and true humanity will rule between the people.

Crystal skulls have changed the lives of many people around the world, helped them with profound transformations and led them to a life in deep love and gratitude.

They allow people to get in contact with the wisdom and the knowledge of thousands of years' history, with cosmic laws and wisdom, as well as with the entire evolutionary history of mother earth; they are gigantic computers that stored our complete past on their hard drive.

There are many different myths dealing with the theory that if a certain amount of ancient skulls (13, 24 or 52) reunite in this world, the world will change to an extent we cannot even imagine, and that nothing will be like we know it. This time of reunification corresponds, according to many prophecies of indigenous people, to our present time.

Crystal skulls unite people in the whole world who are working with them, they create networks that live in a small scale what we all hope for and dream of for this world: love, mutual esteem and respect and harmony.

Since Kasper, my beloved crystal skull, moved in, my life also changed profoundly and many wonderful friendships to crystal skull caretakers in the whole world evolved.

Kasper for me is a partner and friend, guidance, a messenger and also a tool, which I do use in healing sessions with my clients and also in ceremonies and ritual to thank Mother Earth.

He is at my side when I give classes about crystal skull work, he travels with me to sacred sites and he was the one who asked me to write a book about crystal skull work, after I finished the crystal skull card deck.

In Kasper's opinion it is pretty important to offer another vehicle through which people can connect to the multi-dimensional aspects of the crystal skulls.

In these massively transformative times people need help to awaken to their full potential and multidimensional selves.

I believe crystal skulls help us to create a balance between our spiritual being and our ego. We are spirit, exploring physical existence in order to learn and grow.

One of their essential messages is – "Remember who you are. Your origin has become clouded by everyday living. Reclaim your ability to love and support the miracle of life," as Marion Webb-De Sisto said in an interview in my book.

If we live in the knowledge that we are never alone, that all our steps are supported by the divine guidance, it will be much easier for us to go our next steps and to trust that everything that happens in our life is right and helps us growing in order to be able to follow the path of our soul.

Kirsten Hilling
http://www.horus-mystery-school.com
or
http://www.white-buffalo-calf-woman.com
Email: Kirsten@horus-mystry-school.com

CRYSTAL SKULL 10

AKASHIC RECORDS:

What say you regarding Skull 10?
What additional Information is there?

Personal Note - the information was gathered and written on a number 10 day, such synchronicity.

SKULL 10

- I Am Skull 10 the Light of God nestled deep in the Earth.
- I Am Skull 10 the Light of God reflected to Earth in each every cloud.
- I Am Skull 10, the Lightening putting nitrogen in the Earth as a nutrient for the plants.
- I Am Skull 10, the Lightening activating the nitrogen in the Earth as nutrients for all the plants.
- I Am Skull 10 the Language of Light.
- I Am Skull 10 connecting Heaven (the center of the Universe) with the crystalline core of the Earth.
- I Am Skull 10 bringing Light to the microbes, viruses, fungi and bacteria deep within the Telluric Realm.
- I Am Skull 10 bringing the Natural Forest Fires for Balance on Earth. The Spring and Autumn house cleaning.
- I Am Skull 10 All of the Colors of the Language of Light.
- I Am Skull 10 bringing the Vibrations and Frequencies carrying knowledge and wisdom.
- I Am Skull 10 the sine Waves of Quantum physics and Light.
- I Am Skull 10 the Vibrations and Frequencies of Numbers.
- I Am Skull 10 the God Code. Gregg Braden wrote a book called "The God Code, The Secret of Our Past, and the Promise of Our Future."
- I Am Skull 10 my place is in the South on the Medicine Wheel, the place of Fire bringing Light.
- I Am Skull 10 bringing the Light that Illuminates the darkness for expanded conscious awareness.
- I Am Skull 10 revealing the Truth.

- I Am Skull 10, Integrity and Honesty.
- I Am Skull 10 the Illumined One
- I Skull 10 bring Illumination and Enlightenment to All Sentient Beings. When humans receive my Light, they begin to glow.
- I Am Skull 10 the Halo of Light of Illumined Human Beings.
- I Am Skull 10 raising the vibrations of all who receive me.
- I Skull 10 raise the frequencies of all who receive me.
- I Am Skull 10, the beginning of the final Ascension.
- I Am Skull 10 the pioneer with new ideas, new information and new creations
- I Am Skull 10 carrying Knowledge and Wisdom supported by the God head.
- I Am Skull 10 carrying the Language of the Soul from inception to birth, death and rebirth.

The Mayan Calendar:

This calendar does not correlate to the Gregorian or Julian Calendars because of all of the changes and imperfections. The two calendars below are important because the Cholq'ij Calendar and the Ab' Calendar coincide on the same day and number every 52 years.

52 years divided into 4 periods of 13 years each, for a total of 18,980 days – a number equally divisible by 260 and 365. The 52 years results from methodical and constant observation of the Pleiades, which pass through their zenith every 52 years.

The Mayan Medicine Wheel is 52 years divided into 4 periods of 13 years. We have 13 Original Crystal Skulls.

There are 260 days in the Mayan Calendar called Cholq'ij Calendar.

There are 20 Mayan Sun Signs and 13 Galactic Tones. 13 x 20 = 260 Days on the Cholq'ij Calendar and then repeats.

Wayeb = Special 5 days that aren't considered part of the year – it was considered to be a time of fasting, with self-restraint and that work that was absolutely necessary. A time of making offerings to the Great Father (Ajaw) in gratitude for being able to work 360 days. Wayeb is not counted in the baktuns or 400 year periods.

Ab'Kaj = numerical system created to control and manage time based on distance, velocity, and movement. It is Infinite, yet the ancient Mayans never got lost in space because of their skill as visionaries, physicists and mathematicians.

Static Ab' = The Ab' calendar of 365 days = 360 days + 5 days of Wayeb. The year begins with month zero, Po'op. It is 18 months of 20 days each and after 52 years it ends on 0Po'op.

Oxluju Baktun = 5,200 year cycle called the Long Count. It is a system for recording time in a linear manner rather than circular. The formula for the Long Count is:

Q'ij or Kin = 1 day
Winal = 20 days
Tun = 360 days
Katun = 7,200 days or 20 years

Mayan Astrology is based on the cosmic- earthly rhythm. The Mayan Cross with the four main directions and elements – Earth, Air, Fire and Water.

Picture and Medicine Wheel in Part X by Iva Deane Gemmell, The Saga-Oracle Earth = North = White = Winter; Air = East = Red = Spring; Fire = South = Yellow = Summer; Water = West = Black = Autumn. This applicable for North of the Equator for the Mayans, the Apache and the Woodland Nations

The God Code:

This is directly related to the Hebrew Alpha/Numeric System for creation. According to Gregg Braden in his book "The God Code":

A combined value of 26 is precisely the same value held in the ancient name of god – YHVH. Yod = 10 (Aleph =1and The Lord is One). Aleph is made up of two separate letters Yod= 10 + Vav = 6 +10 for God = 26x 10 = 260 corresponding to the Mayan Calendar of Days.

In Nature, the appearance of order described by universal mathematical formulas and numbers of the Golden Mean and the Fibonacci Progression indicate the presence of an Intelligence of Great magnitude. We call that Intelligence God/ Creator/ Great Spirit, etc.

137

Mother + Father are not enough numerically to produce a child Adam the first of our species. Only when God (1) is added is the formula complete.

The Language of Light is also directly related to: Picture Image in Part X.

Word Signs = Hieroglyphs in and on Pyramids in North, Central and South America. This includes the Petroglyphs on canyon walls and in caves.

Different Signs or Symbols represent individual Sounds.

Entire Alphabets (Sanskrit, Hebrew, Chinese, Egyptian, Greek and Mayan) are symbols of the Language of Light.

Symbols and letters translate to numbers, a deeper reality that is universal. The Hebrew Alphabet has 22 letters, all of which have a healing frequency.

The 13 Tones of the Mayan Calendar correspond to the 13 Original Crystal Skulls. Tones have specific frequencies.

Each Human Being has a specific frequency unique to them. It is their DNA Coding. The Language of Light is the Language of our Soul. Each individual has his or her own frequency then it follows that they have a unique sound that is only theirs, called their Soul Sound.

In Egyptian Cosmology – the Sun God is said to have created the Universe with a "CRY OF LIGHT," which seems the most accurate as Sound and Light are connected and both are wave forms.

In scripture it says "First there was the Word," however Light came first in "Let there be Light."

Sound and Light are connected. Sound travels 40 Octaves slower than visible Light. The slowing down of light frequencies produces colors of the rainbow or the visible color spectrum which correspond to the musical scale. (Picture in Part XI)

• *The Color Therapy Program in my Quantum Biofeedback Machine, the SCIO, is flashing color and sound that the individual's DNA has requested to Balance the Amino Acids of the Brain. Amino Acids are one of the building blocks of our physical body. Our DNA is in the Nucleus of each cell. Our DNA has a specific vibration, a unique and specific code for each individual Being.*

138

The specific code of each person allows access to their Akashic Records. Akasha is a Sanskrit word meaning Primordial Substance, the foundation of our DNA and Life as the Language of our Soul; the Language of Light.

Each and every human being is fluent in the Language of the Akasha/the Language of Light at an unconscious level for it is the Language of the Soul.

Carl Jung said *"The man/woman who speaks with primordial images speaks 1000 tongues."*

It is the Light Language translated by the Masters, Teachers and Loved Ones into this Language that can be drawn, read, put into song and it is also transmitted silently in a knowing of pure thought. Its sounds, colors, frequencies and vibrations can heal and change our cellular genetic memory codes, restoring the original DNA blueprint. The symbols that we see, feel, hear and know can stimulate us consciously and at the unconscious level, effecting our emotions with greater speed and at a much deeper level than any spoken language. This can create "miraculous" healings, knowing or "Ah Ha" moments that infuse us with more Light and Sound, raising our Vibration and the amount of Light that we hold, restoring the missing Sounds.

According to Deepak Chopra, when sound or a specific frequency is missing, the body is stressed, "dis-ease" enters. When we restore the Sound we eliminate the stress, health is restored to that area of the body. This can also happen when we use the Therapeutic Grade Oils of the Scripture that have specific Healing Codes, Frequencies and Vibrations.

The way I prefer to teach the Akashic Records is with discernment of frequencies and vibrations using a "teaching prayer" and Light Meditations. With the "teaching prayer" each student receives the personal Akashic Record Prayer and closing; their own Sacred Prayer aligned with their vibration and frequency, increasing the amount of Light they are holding and thus raising their vibrations to be in tune to receive the information, guidance and healing. As we change and grow, our personal Prayer changes. (My Personal Prayer changed twice while writing this book as I raised my vibration).

This is Quantum Healing for it is truly from Source as we send out our prayers, questions, requests – we are sending out waves of Sound and Light without thoughts and the questions we write down.

All Questions are prayers is what I teach in our Shamanic Journey Drum Circles and when I teach people how to access their Akashic Records.

The thoughts and prayers go out as waves of Sound and Light frequencies. These frequencies have numerical values. That is why we can work with the computers at such a high speed because the crystalline chips can process the information with their intelligences. The geometric symbols also have numerical values.

The more Light we shine, the more we can interact with the Planet, the plant and animal kingdoms as well as the microbial kingdom in the telluric realm and the stars and Creator/ God/ Infinite Mind. This communication is with symbols, platonic solids, sacred geometry, pictures and words.

The Language of Light is the parent language of Creator – It is the God Code. It is also known as the Mother tongue or the Language of Angels. Its frequencies are based on UNITY CONSCIOUSNESS, where there are no lower vibration thought forms.

This Language of Light is encoded in the 13 Original Crystal Skulls. The thoughts of the Skulls manifest our world, our reality and the Life forms of the Earth Mother.

That is the purpose of our writing with the Skulls. The Language of Light informs us and we in turn, relate their teachings in words so that the World and beyond can be informed and infused with the God Code.

The Skulls – All of them in different ways are reminding us that we need to realize and know that we are Light Beings and always have been.

Our breath is Spirit. We are able to consciously express ourselves in light particles (quantum). By having intent, we will uplift our cellular vibrations until we are pure beings of Light.

Soul = Light
Spirit = Sound

Together they are the dancing Kundalini up and down our spine – receiving and giving...

As Above So Below and As Below So Above –
The Time is NOW!

140

Shamanic Journeys: Today is 4/11/2011 = 19/10 – One supported by The God Head

What is the Energy of Skull 10?
What is the Information of Skull 10?
What is the Sound of Skull 10?

SOUND:

The Sound of Skull 10 is the Language of Light because God is perfectly expressed in Nature.   The Sound of Skull 10 is the many Sounds of Nature. The rainbow after the rain is speaking the Language of Light. Each color has a symbol and meaning. Each of the first eight colors is aligned with the musical scale and the chakras of the human body.

- Red
- Orange
- Yellow
- Green
- Pink
- Turquoise
- Indigo
- Purple
- Mother of Pearl
- Pure Blue White

ENERGY:

The Energy of Skull 10 is a very bright clear cobalt blue skull with Lightening sparking out of it and off of it. This Skull has many facets as if a Library transmitting information out into the Ethers via Lightening.
Skull 10 is infused with Love as the foundation for radiating Light filled with the information, wisdom and guidance for Healing Cultural and Ancestral Fear.

Skull 10 sheds Light on Woundedness by radiating Light from within connecting to the meridians of Life for a New Beginning of Wholeness.

Skull 10 raises the Vibrations and Frequencies of Every Life Form that receives its Energy and Light strengthening the connection with every other living Being and Intelligence. Light is the conductor and the connector.

141

- I Am, Skull 10 the Conductor of information, feelings, wisdom, knowledge, and guidance from Source/ Creator/ God.
- I, Skull 10 transmit the needs wants and desires only for the Highest and Best Good.
- I, Skull 10 discern and discriminate between the various frequencies and vibrations needed at any given moment.
- I Skull 10 bring Lightening and Illumination; with Illumination comes Enlightenment; with Enlightenment comes the inner frequency of Pure Love.

Pure Love is the Foundation of All that Is.

- I, Skull 10 radiate Lighted Love infused with colors, numbers, sine waves of sound and light, frequencies and vibrations raising the universal consciousness.

Light waves travel so fast that there is no discernible sound to the Human Ear. Sound travels 40 Octaves slower than Light as discussed in the Language of Light. If there is a sound at the higher frequencies for Humans to hear – it is with symbols. The star, the cross, the quarter moon, the flag are all recognized symbols. The symbol of a double helix – then an additional double helix radiating more light; the halos around people and in paintings from the pineal tubes; the radiating Light from the eyes; the brightness of the colors they choose for their feathers, fur, scales, the glow of a tree.

People so moved by feeling and emotion will start speaking in Tongues. So at a lower audible frequency, speaking in Tongues is the voice of Source/Creator's/ God's Light coming through Skull 10.

The plants – all plants carry the Language of Light in their blood, their essence. When these plant parts are distilled properly the liquid becomes Therapeutic Grade Essential Oils. Each Essential Oil has a frequency and vibration that heals spiritually, emotionally, mentally and physically. There is a plant for balancing, reversing and healing any condition. These pure Therapeutic Grade Oils are Alive with an electromagnetic field. They also operate at as Quantum Healers receiving the intention and prayers for healing.

Animals communicate and speak the Language of Light. They see the Light, the Electromagnetic fields of Light around each Being and Intelligence. The Sounds of Nature are part of the Languages of Light for Creator/ God is perfectly expressed in Nature.

On May 4, 2011 – Linda Howe Founder of The Center for Akashic Studies released a new definition of the Akashic Records, as discussed earlier. This is another confirmation and acknowledgement of the Language of Light which is inherent in each living Being and Intelligence in the Universe.

Everything Vibrates – Everything is connected to Source in cycles and waves of leaving and returning, up and down, in and out.

CRYSTAL SKULL 11

Akashic Records: It is April 11, 2011 = the 11th day of the 11th year – a portal day.

What say you regarding Skull 11?
What additional Information do you have for us?

We are Star Beings made Manifest on and in the Earth.

The iron of meteorites is my core. And, although, I am not physically present in the third dimension vision of your Earth walk, I AM ever present.

- The 11, the two ones or two poles are always receiving the continual flow of Light and Love from the Heavens, the Stars and from the Earth.
- I Am Skull 11, a multi-dimensional Being.
- I Am Skull 11, I bring peace, serenity, compassion and calm from the Stars who have had tumultuous pasts and solved their differences with their families, neighbors, friends and associates on their planets on their stars and with their planetary neighbors.
- I Am Skull 11, I bring clearing.
- I Am Skull 11, I bring renewal. The clearing and renewal comes from the Pleiades, Sirius, and Andromeda and from stars yet to be named.
- I Am Skull 11 Unformed and Informed Fluid Energy carried on the Love Frequency. In the fluidity is much information for releasing and receiving.
- I, Skull 11 clear the old in a kind and loving way with my Waters.
- I, Skull 11 make room for the higher vibrations and frequencies of Illumined Peace.
- I, Skull 11 transform and transmute to a Loving existence where ever Beings work together in Harmony and synchronicity.
- I Am Skull 11, who clears the final vestiges of Fear and Doubt.
- I, Skull 11 leave only Illumination of the wonderful Uniqueness of each Being and Intelligence Connected to All others in the Web of Life; in Peace and Harmony.
- I Am Skull 11 (1+1=2)
- I Am Skull 11, I Am from the Stars formed in the Heavens

144

- I Am Skull 11 and I am in the Earth radiating a fluid flow of Energy, but I AM Not of the Earth.
- I Am Skull 11, the Flow – Involution and Evolution.

Additional Information – Chevron Amethyst (see picture in Part XI)

The additional information came from Research I was told to do on Chevron Amethyst   Crystal in the book "Love Is In the Earth – A Kaleidoscope Of Crystals" by Melody.

Let us start with what a Chevron is:

1. It is a V-shaped Symbol, especially one used as a sign of rank on military and police uniforms.
2. It is a Heraldic Ornament, a heraldic in the form of a wide inverted V-shape = ^
3. It is a Star-gate a portal device within the Star-gate "fictional" universe that allows practical, rapid travel between two distant locations.

Internet Research reveals the following information Professionally Researched by Mollye Miller on April 24, 2011.

This great answer was researched and sourced by a professional writer, as well as copy-edited and fact checked by a professional copy-editor. This isn't a replacement for the combined knowledge of our tremendous community — it's an addition! We hope you'll find these professionally researched answers useful, and it will encourage you to ask and answer even more!

Word Origin:

The French word "chevron" means rafter, the sloping supporting beam that runs from the ridge beam of a roof to its edge.

Symbolism:

The chevron image showing a roof-peak on a house symbolizes protection.

History:

In feudal times during the Middle Ages (circa 1066 to 1485) knights and men-at-arms received the "top of the house" chevron badge or shield as an emblem of rank. Knights carried the chevron symbol on their shields in battle.
Chevron Amethyst is used for clearing the aura and to release tension.

It is excellent for inner journeying. We will look at both Amethyst and Chevron Amethyst, which builds on the properties of amethyst. Amethyst vibrates at 3 and Chevron Amethyst vibrates at 7 and number 11 all sit in the same direction, West on the Mayan Medicine Wheel.

Native legends speak of crystal skulls as an inheritance from ancient times. Said to "talk and sing" they are believed to carry messages for all mankind, including what may be discovered when we overcome our fear of death.

- I Am Crystal Skull 11 and with the other Singing Crystal Skulls, we are tools of awareness and we assist each individual being to:
  Focus Energy
  Reflect Energy
  Attune Energy
  Transmit Energy
  Transform Energy
  Store Energy
  Amplify Energy

Again, Chevron Amethyst is used for clearing the aura and to release tension. It is excellent for inner journeys.

Amethyst Information:

- Amethyst Crystal is a stabilizing energy, thought to assist in learning to trust your connection to the Divine and acknowledge the Guidance received.
- Amethyst also supports and assists in stopping self-abuse. It brings calm, inner peace, courage and balance. It has been used to protect against psychic attacks.
- Amethyst is associated with the third eye and the crown chakras.
- Amethyst is used as protection for travelers.
- Amethyst is associated with Angels and is an excellent stone for meditation, dream work, or past life work.
- Amethyst is a stone for releasing and transmuting energies.
- Amethyst has also been used to help ease the pain of grief.
- Amethyst is reputed to be useful when working through money issues and legal problems. It's often been called a stone of prosperity and abundance.
- Amethyst is said to beneficial when overcoming any kind of addiction. It is also used for compulsive behaviors as well as addictions of all kinds.
- Amethyst has much higher vibrations for mental, emotional and spiritual healing. These properties are:

- It is a stone of spirituality and contentment.
- It facilitates transmutation of lower frequencies into spiritual and ethereal levels or vibrations.
- It represents the principles of complete metamorphosis.
- It balances the energies of the physical, intellectual, emotional and spiritual bodies.
- It provides a clear connection between the Earth plane and other worlds of existence in the Universe.
- It bestows stability, strength, and invigoration and peace – the peace present prior to birth – the perfect peace of the higher realms.
- It is the stone of meditation.
- It opens and activates the crown chakra.
- It can be used against psychic attacks.
- It transmutes the energy of the psychic attacks then transmits it into the Universe as positive, loving energy.
- It enhances cooperation and co-creation between a humans four body of experience, between the physical and spiritual worlds and affairs of this world.
- It encourages flexibility in decision making while providing calm to clear away unproductive and unkind vibrations.
- It assists in the assimilation of new ideas, new ways of thinking, new ways of being, raising the state of consciousness.

According to Melody the Amethyst Chevron crystal has All Astrological Signs as its Sun sign. It is of the variety exhibiting on of the deepest purple hue. These stones are found in Siberia and India.

The Attributes with brief description of the Amethyst Chevron are:

- It has all of the properties of Amethyst as described above.
- The energies allow it to be represented as one of the finest third eye stones, stimulating vision into unknown realms deep within the Self and into the Universe and beyond.
- It enhances the perception of the aura. The forceful yet subtle rays provide for clearing of the aura and for the release and dissipation of negativity. After the cleansing, one can, literally become absorbed in its radiance.
- It further stimulates the "higher" aspect of each individual Being and encouraging the emanating warmth and the purity of love within ones being.
- When placed on individual chakras, it serves to release tensions of that chakra.
- It further energizes the areas that have been static and stagnant.
- It is an excellent stone for journeying.

147

- It is the stone for inner-soul/self-evaluation and evolution.
- It gives one the strength and loving essence to preserver in any and all pursuits.
- It is energy is for psychic research – assisting one in transporting and retrieving patterns of force, movement and time-space relationships.
- It allows one to trace negative energies to their source providing information, reasons for and origins so they can be transmuted.
- It stimulates understanding of positive answers and solutions to any problem.
- It assists one in the selection of the best solution of the highest good relative to a Being's purpose and to the doctrine of universal love.
- It helps actualize what is required for personal, planetary and universal growth and development.
- It furthers one's acceptance of unseen forces which are available to complete the thoughts and actions that create a perfect state.
- It helps with the application of central unity to all of existence.
- It aids one in understanding the abstract forms of one's being and the total release of resistance.

The Chevron Amethyst has a larger force field that can affect a greater area and can stimulate cooperation between various members of a family, group or countries, bringing balance to the community structure. In a much larger arena, Crystal Skull11 does the same thing on a Universal level.

Shamanic Journeys:

What is the Energy of Skull 11?
What information does Skull 11 have to share today?
What is the Sound of Skull 11?

Hello, I Am Skull 11, I sit in the West the home of the Waters that nourish;
The Waters that purify and clear.

- I Am the Skull of $11 = 2$. I AM two (2) at a higher vibration. I Am beyond 7.
- I Am 11, each side a perfect reflection of the other. It represents equilibrium between two extremes.
- I Am an 11 the first Master Number.
- I Am ILLUMINATION which says "Shine the Lighted Love across the Land and into the Universe."
- I Am the Hollow Bone receiving God's Love and Light to transmute and heal old thought forms.

148

- I Am Mother of Pearl – iridescent colors formed from a wound; the precious pearl born from a grain of sand.
- I Am Skull 11; I Am a Heavenly Being in the Earth, not of the Earth.

SOUND:

On Earth, I Am the sound of Rainstorms with Thunder and Lightning – All Healing, Energizing and Renewing.

The Earth is renewed by Thunder Storms. I Am the Home of the Thunder Beings – The bowling alley of heaven that follows the Lightening.

ENERGY:

- I Am the Waters of the Moon working in Harmony and Love with the Waters of the Earth as expressed with the Oceans, Seas, Lakes, Rivers, Streams, Creeks, Wetlands and Estuaries and in the Blood of all Sentient Beings and Plants.
- As Skull 11, my Energy is very fluid always flowing as if between the river banks or the unseen currents of the Oceans and Lakes.
- I Am the Undercurrents of All bodies of Water.
- I Am Skull 11; I Am the embodiment of ever flowing Love. I Am continually clearing, cleaning and restoring all who choose to communicate with me.
- I Am Skull 11, I Love touching in to feel your flow and I Love soothing and smoothing out the jagged edges and spikes of your energy field.
- I AM Skull 11; I enjoy bringing the soothing Love and Serenity of a flowing stream to each individual Being and Intelligence.
- I Am the Skull of Peace and Calm and of Compassion and Serenity.
- I Am the place where you can float in nothingness and everything.
- I Am Skull 11; I Am the last Skull in the West on the Medicine Wheel, where the final healing has occurred. The Transmutation of your thoughts leads to the Transformation of your entire Being – A Quantum Healing.

Moldavite: (Picture in Part XI) Moldavite is only found in Czech Republic.

The stone Moldavite represents numbers 11/2. It is a 15 million year old beautiful green stone that is the rarest variety of gem quality tektite of extra-terrestrial origin.

Moldavite is also the Stone and Energy of Skull 11. It allows direct access to higher dimensional galactic Energies.

149

According to Melody in her book "Love is in the Earth" Moldavite is a stone to serve the inhabitants of Earth. It serves to promote cooperation with extra-terrestrials and those experiencing life on this planet. It carries one beyond the Illusion of Life to a home from which one has been absent.

- Moldavite provides the image of eternity as well as the vision and energy to translate that image into reality.
- Moldavite draws into the Earth plane those thought patterns and Light Vibrations that are optimal for preparing for Illumination and Ascension.
- Moldavite facilitates strong, clear and direct multidimensional interconnected-ness between one's consciousness and the higher planes of Light.
- Moldavite expands the scope and magnitude of the vibrational spectrums that can be accessed while providing clarity and willingness to "see."
- Moldavite expands the vibrational range of existing vision and provides an interconnection to the other dimensional horizons not yet experienced.
- Moldavite works through the crown chakra, the third-eye and throat chakra.

Skull 11 and Moldavite are extra-terrestrial and carry messages and visions for new ways of being in balance and expanding our consciousness.

Skull 11 – More Akashic Record Information on April 30, 2011 = 4+ 30+4 = 38/11/2

What Additional Information is there on Skull 11?

In conversations with your shaman after your "Soul Retrieval" you talked about electropiezo crystals. That is what we are – electropiezo crystal. We, all of the Skulls, are vast Libraries of Knowledge that you have just begun to explore. Each one of us has many books about the mysteries within us.

- I Am Skull 11, the Skull of Transmutation and Transformation.

You, Marilee had to experience your own transformation before you were able to move forward with your writing about us. Even more transformations happened and were experienced between this 4/30/11 and today 3/31/13, twenty six months later and more transformations have occurred as you prepare to have your paperback published.

All is in Divine Order of the Universe. This is an important concept for Everyone to remember!

The Electropiezo Crystal is the Communicator of Sound, Images and the Language of Light that uplifts or destroys.

Our purpose in the transformation process is to destroy that which no longer serves. It is important to be fully aware of the phrase *"that which no longer serves."*

This awareness is what makes Quantum Healing possible whether it is with Soul Retrieval, Shamanic Counseling, Vision Quest, the QXCI/SCIO, Reiki, Prayer or any other Energy Healing Modality.

Transmutation and Transformation is Quantum Healing. By definition, Quantum Healing is "Healing from Source" for each individual Being and Intelligence.

Transmutation and Transformation are Change.

- Change in your thinking,
- Change in your feeling,
- Change in your perception,
- Change in your levels of awareness.

The only difference between Masters and Students is the former have let go of *"That Which No Longer Serves."*

Releasing the old and raising your vibration by being receptive to what is being offered that changes "Stinking Thinking" as they say in AA (Alcoholics Anonymous) programs?

Transformation is about re-writing the software programs in each individual brain and activating the Pineal Gland at the top of the head – the Crown Chakra. The Pineal Gland is each individual's "Electropiezo Crystal." At the age of maturity in mammals; the Pineal Gland begins transmuting and transforming into an Electropiezo Crystal. In humans that process begins at about age 18.

Quantum Healing is Miraculous Healing from the "Ah Ha" moments of increased awareness with responsibility taken by the person receiving the "Ah Ha".

The Electropiezo Crystal is the Mid or Center Chakra and it is the Receiving and Transmitting Station of each individual human. This is the point in our Physical Body System where we receive the information and knowing from

151

All That Is/ the Universe/ Source/ Creator/ Great Mystery/ Great Spirit/ God –
the One known by a 1000 names.

The number 11 and Skull 11 represent the Psychic, the Visionary and the
Dreamer because their Pineal Gland is fully activated. Their Intuition and
Knowing is magnified by the vibratory force of 11, enhancing the attributes of
the number 2. Sensitivity; Creative Visualization; Creativity and Originality
are all greatly increased and amplified.

Skull 11 enhances the connection between All That Is and Humans.

All humans have the spark of "God" within them. The Pineal raises that
awareness with Transmutation and Transformation of Awareness and
Perception of the Lighted Love and the connection with All That Is including
All Life on Earth.

People in fear have a very difficult time perceiving beyond themselves. The
level of awareness is limited.

This is obvious in the politics of the USA, the Middle East and the World at
Large. Republicans and Democrats in USA are different – one group is in fear
and "hawkish" and one group wants to help everyone and change the world.

In the Middle East, the Dictators live in fear of losing "power" (which is only
a perception) to those people that want freedom and the "power" to think and
know for themselves, to have their own opinions. They want to be able to
express their uniqueness and originality.

There is no room for fanaticism or fear in this process.

Transmutation and Transformation can only happen with great difficulty when
fear rules.

Skull 11 increases sensitivity and allows for "diplomacy" (The ability to see
both sides is increased) and creative solutions where everyone "wins" for the
Highest and Best Good of All That Is. Peace and Calm prevail with
Compassion and Serenity.

CRYSTAL SKULL 12

Akashic Records

What say you regarding Skull 12?
What additional Information is there?

Skull 12 sits in the North on the Medicine Wheel; it is the completed circle.

$1 + 2 = 3$, the holy trinity – the triangulated energy amplifying the messages from the Universe, from Source. This is the Visioning Place for New Ways of Living; New Group Structures.

It is $4 + 4 + 4$ making it a manifesting number with the God Source. It incorporates all that came before it. It is where transmutation and transformation manifest with Source/Creator supported by the Lords of Light and the Masters, Teachers and Loved Ones of the Akashic Records that correspond to the knowledge of Crystal Skull 12.

- I Am Skull 12, a guide book for manifesting at the highest levels of existence as the Universe expands, experiencing itself on all of the Planets.
- I Skull 12 expand my information and knowledge from the Universe and transmit that body of information to the other Skulls.
- I Skull 12 receive questions from the other Skulls and relay those questions, prayers and requests to the Universe and wait for the response I Am to transmit.
- I Am Skull 12, the Galactic Communicator.
- I Am Skull 12 I bring forth new thought forms and symbols.
- I Am Skull 12 I expand the Language of Light.
- I Skull 12 communicate with the Ascended Masters and I AM Presence to bring Light and Information to the Iron Crystal Core of the Earth.
- I Am Skull 12 of the 12th Dimension.
- I Skull 12 have normal conversations and discourse with what humans call "aliens." It is acceptable and in line with our function to talk, discusses ideas and share our knowledge and wisdom with one another. It is the same as talking with Humans and All the Beings of the Earth.

153

- I Am Skull 12 the Wisdom Keeper of the Universe.
- I Am Skull 12 the Visionary of the Universe.
- I Am Skull 12 the Wisdom Keeper for Pleiades, Sirius, Andromeda, Arcturus and beyond to include the Sun and the Great Central Sun, Mars, Mercury, Earth, Venus, Saturn, Jupiter, Neptune, Pluto and all of the configurations of stars in the zodiac – 12 or 13 star systems depending on your belief system.
- I Am Skull 12 the Wisdom Keeper for all of the Star Systems
- I Am Skull 12 the Visionary for All of these Systems and their respective Life forms, Beings and Intelligences
- I Am Skull 12 the Vision Keeper for Each of these Beings and Intelligences.
- I Am Skull 12 the Vision Keeper for Each Star, Star System, Planets, individual Beings and Intelligences down to the smallest microbe
- I Skull 12 correspond and communicate with the Lords of the Akasha and the Board of Karma for the Galaxy to create a brighter future for All – not just the Earth and her inhabitants.

All "new" Technology comes through me, Skull 12, first based on decisions made by the Galactic Board of Karma.

All "new" Inventions for the Expansion of Awareness and Consciousness come through me, Skull 12. This is how I work with Earthlings.

Know that what you call your Akashic Records are in fact those and so much more. I work with and help the Lords of the Akashic Records discern what information comes through in an understandable way. In working with me, Skull 12, your Akashic Record Prayers for Access will change and I look forward to your direct "Journeys" to me.

A Personal Note:

The colors of the energy coming in did change and so did my Prayer. My prayer has greatly expanded. When I sat down and opened my Records with my January 8, 2010 Prayer the colors had shifted and I had attributed that to a Soul Retrieval that I had received. Also to work with these higher vibrations, the Prayer's Vibration had to increase dramatically and during the final edit when I got to Skull 10 it changed again.

The guidance was to also expand my Teaching Prayer. The Prayer was expanded to include the Crystal Skulls. (This will be in Book II of the trilogy call Prayer and Meditation).

What is really interesting to me is how the Skulls build one on the other. As we worked with the various Skulls we, too, had to expand our awareness and receive healings so that we opened up our consciousness and awareness to receive the information in a good way. We trusted the information we received.

- I Am Skull 12; I Am far beyond religion.

Spirituality Creates and Expands with Lighted Love.

Religion creates fear in earthlings.
Religion is not for Spiritual growth.
Religious Dogma stifles.

Shamanic Journeys:

What is Your Energy of Skull 12?
What is Your Information, Skull 12?
What is Your Sound Skull 12?

Personal Note:

It is interesting that the questions changed to add Sound. We completed Skulls 11 and 12 on April 30, 2011 = 38/11. This was an 11 day for Transmuting and Transforming. We then went back to receive the Sound for Each of the other Skulls.

SOUND:

I Am Skull 12 and my Sound is the Sound of the Big Bang; the Sound of the Universe expanding. The Human Ear is unable to hear my actual sound. You hear Silence. Yet it is a loud explosion – The Big Bang opening to other universes, planets, dimensions and worm holes.

ENERGY:

The Energy of Skull 12, in my journey, looks like the Black Void surrounded by a Circle of Bright White Light with Rays emanating in all directions (a black circle surrounded by a Circle of Light Rays.).

- I Am Skull 12 and my color is actually deep dark indigo blue/royal purple almost black velvet surrounded by Light. The description above is quite accurate because of the depth in color of the blue/purple often looks

155

like the black void. Think of dark rich soft velvet that shifts from blue to black to purple to dark blue to black and back again always surrounded by rays of light, like a crown.

- I Am Skull 12 with 52 spokes of Informing Light emanating from me. One spoke for each year of the Medicine Wheel. Each beam of Light is filled with the Language of Light at a different frequency.

The Light is Information, Pure Knowledge, Wisdom, Healing, Technology for Healing and the Greater Good, Inventions for the Greater Good and New Ways of Being.

Each spoke corresponds to one year in the quadrant where it is located on the Circle/ Medicine Wheel of my Being. In human life span terms: See diagram in Part XI.

The East represents ages 1 to 13. East is the Home of Skulls 1, 5, and 9.
The South represents ages 13 to 26. South is the Home of Skulls 2, 6 and 10
The West represents ages 26 to 39. West is the Home of Skulls 3, 7, and 11
The North represents ages 39 to 52. North is the Home 4, 8 and 12

- I Am Skull 12, a multi-dimensional being.
- I Am Skull 12 - I look like a star in deep space with Light beams filled with the Language of Light shooting out in all directions.
- I Am Skull 12 with deep dark indigo/purple openings between the beams of Light to receive from All parts of the Universe and beyond.
- I Am Skull 12 - I Am androgynous and perfectly balanced – receiving and giving.
- I Am Skull 12 the Home of the Lords of the Akasha.
- I Am Skull 12 the Home the Boards of Karma.
- I Am Skull 12 the Home the Ascended Masters and the Great White Brotherhood.
- I Am Skull 12 an Angel. My partners are Archangel Metatron, Keeper of the Akashic Records and Melchizedek. We work with Archangel Michael, Maitreya and Mary (in all of her forms as their feminine counterpart), with any Being who needs their help, care and power.
- I Am Skull 12 in conjunction with All of my partners in the Universe, we determine what Species, Beings, and Intelligences need to be Seeded and Where for the Greater Good as guided by the Lords of Light and All That Is/ God/Source/Creator.
- I Am Skull 12 and with my partners we work with Beings and Intelligences from the Entire Universe and the Multiverse.

156

- I Am Skull 12 and with my partners we determine which Species, Beings, and Intelligences will be endangered or become endangered for the Greater Good.
- I Am Skull 12 and with my partners we determine which Species, Beings, and Intelligences will disappear for the Greater Good.
- I Am Skull 12 and with my partners, we supervise the University called Earth as well as Venus, Mars, and Mercury and beyond.
- I Am Skull 12 and with my partners, we are in constant Communication with the entire Universe and Beyond as well as with God/Source/Creator. This includes Orion, Arcturus, the Southern Cross, the Big Dipper and the North Star.
- I Am Skull 12 and my partners, supervise the return to Earth those Masters that want to assist in the expansion of consciousness, awareness, perception and knowledge.

The Masters that want to return come as Light-workers to enlighten by sharing ALL of the Love, Knowledge and Wisdom of the Mystery Schools. Nothing will be kept secret. Everything is to be revealed.

The Time Is Now!

- I Am Skull 12: I Am pure Spirit, an Angel, a Messenger.
- I Am Skull 12: I live in all dimensions through all time and space of Earth and beyond.
- I Am Skull 12: I Am the Grand Communicator – Multi-lingual beyond the comprehension of the human mind.
- I Am Skull 12 whose greatest happiness is laughter in conjunction with Change. Change involves contraction and expansion; death and birth on a Universal Level.
- I Am Skull 12: I Am the supervisor for the birth and death of Mars.
- I Am Skull 12: I Am responsible for the Solar Flares that are coming to Earth to accelerate the changes needed on Earth.
- I Am Skull 12: I Am responsible for changing the human consciousness and awareness.
- I Am Skull 12: I Am responsible for the change and destruction, teaching the people of Earth to have Faith and Trust in themselves.
- I Am Skull 12: I Am responsible for teaching that NO government in any country will save humanity. This is true for all Western Nations, Oil Dynasties, Dictatorships and all Multi-National Corporations perpetuating greed and fear.
- I Am Skull 12, with my partners, I allow the manifestation of their worst fears (corporations, governments, dictatorships and the Western Nations) by creating mass chaos. The chaos will get worse during the few years

before the "100th Monkey" affect Informs and Enlightens all humans with Faith, Hope and Trust informed by Loving Communities of friends and families that all resonate together...Tribal and Shamanic in Nature.

- I Am Skull 12, working closely with my Universal Partners and we, as a team, work very closely with Skull 13 – The Alpha and The Omega; The Beginning and The End.

CRYSTAL SKULL 13

AKASHIC RECORDS: May 2, 2011 = 5 + 2 + 4 = 11/2, An 11/2 Day, it is another of Transmuting and Transforming Belief Systems and Ways of Being.

What say you regarding Skull 13?
What Additional information is there?

- I Am Skull 13 - The Alpha and the Omega; the beginning and the end.
  (As a side note, in Aztec Cosmology there are 13 heavens and 13 Skulls in Mayan Cosmology.)
- I Am Skull 13: I represent the Oneness of All That Is.
- I Am Skull 13: I Am the Messenger of Love.
- I Am Skull 13: I Am the Knowing and beyond... All things All Beings and All Intelligences are Love.
  (It takes great Courage for an angel, a messenger of Source/Creator, to lower its vibration to come to Earth to be of Planetary Service. All of Skulls are of Planetary Service in specific areas of teaching and information that is within each individual Skull.)
- I Am Skull 13: I encompass all of the information of All 13 Skulls in Onement.
- I Am Skull 13: I work directly with the Higher Power of the Universe and beyond.
- I Am Skull 13 the Zero Chakra.
  The Zero Chakra is the cervix to the Earth. It is also the cervix for each mammal, for each individual Being/Intelligence as it is the point of conception on and in the Earth, the eggs, in the wombs moving upward multiplying the cells into its particular life form.
  Zero Chakra is also the entry point of Light/Life Force and the exit point of Love for the Individual Being/Intelligence
- I Am Skull 13,
- I Am the Skull that corresponds with all the actual Chakra numbers; I correspond to the Zero Chakra in the Earth and the 13th Chakra in the Heavens.

Moving on, Chakra 1 is everyone's connection to the Earth, her Family and Community. We are working together to be in Onement through this energy of family and community. It is truly about Family groups working together for survival, there is not much leeway for individual expression. Fun is group fun in Gatherings, Ceremonies and Rituals.

Moving upward, Chakra 2 is the Creative Center where if one is open, they can create what makes their heart sing with passion. In creating good food, music, art, writing, the higher realms are brought down through the heart into the body as the foundation of individual expression of Life on Earth. Spirituality fully expressed in all creative expression in partnership with All That Is. At a high vibration, Creative ways of Living originate here. Here we create time to savor Life, to savor the food and wine, to savor love making, to savor the gardens we so lovingly planted with the Co-Creative forces of Nature. To savor the beauty of the Earth whether a beach or mountaintop, forest or desert. In the Natural World there are no "jobs"; no "work". This is the place of co-creation.

Moving upward, we bring you the great golden Central Sun into your Solar Plexus, Chakra 3, and the emotional center. The passion, Love of Life and all that entails balancing the lower vibrational feelings that arise and releasing them into the Onement yet again – pushing out the Light, the higher vibrations through Solar Plexus creating a safe space for your Soul and Spirit to dwell on Earth.

Chakra 4 is the largest Chakra of the Earth Plane Chakras; the one that needs the most healing. The Heart Chakra encompasses your hands, arms, lungs, chest to the heart – the four chambers of the heart as well as the two parts of the chakra itself. Pink is the color of the High Heart of Serenity and Green is the color of The Heart of Love; where the true wisdom and knowledge enter when in Onement. This is where your Akashic Records anchor in as your fetus begins to develop; your Heart develops even before your brain is completely developed. There is a second brain in your Heart that came first.

Chakra 5 is in the Throat, Mouth, and lower Ears. This is where we hear and have our voice, where each individual Being speaks their truth from their Heart and Soul (Solar Plexus). When we are in Onement, there is only an honoring of each individual being with no judgment – Only Acceptance.

Chakra 6 is your bright headlight in the center of your forehead and includes your upper Ears and your physical Eyes. The place where you expand your sight to include the subtle vibrations and frequencies of The Milky Way and everything in it, the waves of light coming off of the hot desert floor, the auras around trees, plants, animals and people, the elves and fairies and All That Is. Your True Sight is here with your Hearing. This is the home of your clairvoyance, clairaudience and clairsentience.

Chakra 7 is your phone line to the Universe. This is the place of exchange, where information and communication from All That Is enters your physical body, heart and mind. It is also the exit point for your heart felt prayers and questions. The 7th Chakra is actually the Center Chakra, with six above and six below. It is the point of communication; the transmitting station, receiving and transmitting information to and from the Universe. It is the point where Shamans launch themselves to travel the inner Earth and the Multiverses.

Chakra 8 is 18 inches above your head. Chakra 8 is the Crossroads. Your physical body is located in the lower circle of the 8. The lower circle of the 8 is the Earth plane of existence for each individual being. As the crossroads, this Chakra acts as the traffic cop modulating the traffic flow of knowledge, guidance, wisdom and information carried on the Light and Sound Waves. Flow is modulated for ease of being and maintaining life and growth on Earth. Heaven enters your Energy Field here.

Chakra 9 is your connecting point to the other planets, the stars, other star systems, the Milky Way, The Universe and Multiverses. It is where your physical body ends and you are only Spirit and Soul in Union. Completing as you prepare to explore new worlds and ways of being.

Chakra 10 is where your Soul and Spirit in Union merge with the waves of Sound and Light, traveling far and wide while maintaining the connection to your body with your Silver and Gold Chords. You use the Language of Light to report situations and to receive the guidance to heal and solve the relationship and creative challenges that you are experiencing in the moment.

Chakra 11 is the point of transformation of existence and being. This is truly where change begins and travels downward into your body. Many people do not go beyond the lower Earth Chakras. This is the Upper reaches of an individual's Tree of Life.

The Earth, herself is a Tree of Life with all of the same chakras and the continual flow of energy from the Heavens to her beautiful round Earthly Body.

Chakra 12 is 12 and the Medicine Wheel is complete. The future plans are held here and released as each individual being is ready, including Earth

161

herself. And, the final choices for each Earth walk or Era are made here. This is the last point before going Home.

Chakra 13 is The Alpha and the Omega, All That Is from zero (0) to 13; it is the beginning and the end. It is Home to your Soul and Spirit. This is where God's Love is made manifest in you and where you shall return. This is Home.

- I Am Skull 13, the Alpha and the Omega.
- I Am Skull 13 the place where Source's Love is made manifest in every living being and intelligence in the Universe and Multiverses.

Number 13 Discussion:

Before we go to the Shamanic Journey information, we are going to discuss the number 13, a much maligned number that is actually extremely powerful because of the numerology.

It is a one (1) and three (3) = four (4) a much higher vibratory level that is directive, active, outward moving and dynamic in nature.

The One (1) is for Leadership and Spirit of "blazing new trails" and three (3) is for healing, self-expression with drive and four (4) is the foundation, the number for the Earth.

In the USA, we have the original 13 colonies, the 13 stripes of our flag.

As 13, the four (4) brings forth evolutionary qualities of awareness, values, ethics and conscience through the Oracle archetype. This is a number for discernment of "right and wrong". It (13) is NOT an unlucky number, but one that requires simultaneous centering and delicate sensitivity to boundaries.

Number 13 is the foundation stone of cosmic law and to awakening each individual's conscience. It symbolizes the 12 Apostles around your "Christ Self." It is your capacity to stand in the center of 12 qualities and harmonize the differences with conscience.

Number 13 is Cosmic Law acting within your own conscience.

Shamanic Journeys:

Skull 13, what is Your Energy?

Skull 13, what is your Sound?
Skull 13, what information do you choose to share today?

I Am Skull 13 I am the "Healer" that brings everyone and everything into Onement.
I Am Skull 13 and I Am Love. Love is the highest of Vibrations. My vibration alone Heals.

(When High vibrations are combined with the young Living Therapeutic Grade Essential Oils (God's Love made manifest through plants and trees) that you use, the affect is amplified and accelerated. The vibrations of the Young Living Oils are so high because they are alive, filled with healing energy. Because the oils are alive and have very complex chemical constituents, they operate at the Quantum Level. They are part of the Quantum Healing Spectrum that I use daily and to help me with this writing and my other "work").

- I Am Skull 13 the Skull of Love.
- I Am Skull 13: I work with All Energetic Healing Modalities that raise vibrations, releasing and healing.
- I Am Skull 13 I Heal with:
Sound with the Shaman's Drum and all Sounds that allow anyone to travel on the waves of Sound and Light
- I Heal with Soul Retrieval, Extraction, and Power Animal/ Totem Retrieval
- I Heal with Energy in the form of Reiki, Quantum Touch, Healing Touch, etc.
- I Heal with Homeopathy
- I Heal with Flowers and Flower Essences. Loving Spirits enter the World through Flowers.
- I Heal with the Elements, Elementals and Fairies of the Earth
- I Heal with the Entire Crystalline Realm
- I Heal with Ceremony and Ritual
- I Heal with Prayer
- I Heal with All Things Loving.

There are 13 Attributes of Love – the six you learned in your Akashic Class from Linda Howe, the two that you were guided to add and now we will add five more attributes. It is important to work with Love as it has so many benefits on the personal level, family level, friend level and local community level, planetary level and beyond.

163

Love is the True Glue holding the Universe together in the precise planetary rhythms and cycles of all things.

Although courage and strength are not specifically listed as attributes of Love, it takes great courage to "keep pushing the envelope" and in your culture in America, it takes great strength to speak our Truth and stand firm in our beliefs when they go against mainstream "normal."

There is a great paradox regarding the Attributes of Love, before we can practice them with others, we must give them to ourselves first then live them, then demonstrating these attributes to others.

That Is the Paradox – Give Love to Ourselves First

The Attributes of Love are:

- Trust
- Forgiveness
- Respect
- Compassion
- Kindness
- Patience
- Generosity
- Gratitude

These are the 8 you have been working with, however to achieve Onement, we must add:

- Abundance
- Acceptance
- Awareness
- Contentment
- Grace

Abundance is on the list of Attributes because Abundance is about being in the flow, knowing that You Deserve all that the Universe has to offer You. Contrary to the lies perpetrated by mass media, this is a very Abundant Universe.

There is No Scarcity or Lack. When you are in Flow, You have Everything You Need.

- Abundance is being in touch with and accessing your 13 Chakras and their attributes.
- Abundance is being part of a Family of Friends.
- Abundance is Being Creative, full of creativity.
- Abundance is being able to Shine Your Light.
- Abundance is being Serene – at Peace.
- Abundance is being able to communicate your authentic self clearly.
- Abundance is being able to see beyond the 3rd Dimension.
- Abundance is being aware of being a receiving and transmitting station.
- Abundance is being the crossroads of flow with Heaven in your body.
- Abundance is being connected to everything in the Milky Way.
- Abundance is being connected to the entire Universe and beyond.
- Abundance is being able to fly into deep space and into the depths of Earth.
- Abundance is being an Agent of Change for the Greater Good – A Transformer.
- Abundance is being Accepted completely for who you are by you.
- Abundance is being able to Manifest your heart's desires.
- Abundance is being able to Heal your Self.
- Abundance is being Whole and Holy.
- Abundance is being in Onement with All that Is.
- Abundance is Being LOVE – that is Abundance in the truest sense of the word Love.

I Am Skull 13; I Am the Rose; I Am Love.

My Energy is a rainbow of colors coming through prisms. My eyes are all seeing and knowing.

- I Am Skull 13, the Wise One holding the Lantern high; I am shedding Light on the Path.
- I Am Skull 13: I am the crystalline core of the Earth and I am deep Space.

Energy:

- I Am Skull 13, my energy is clear purplish blue white light with hints of clear pink.

As Skull 13, I Am multi-dimensional in the truest sense and I often bi-locate to communicate and help people and places.

(Dear Marilee, I work with you often, especially in your dream time and when you are working. I have been working with you for many years. In the future, work directly with me. As Skull 13, I encompass all the elements, the Akashic Records and All That Is.)

Sound:

- I Am Skull 13 and my Sound is all audible sound that soothes and heals.
- I Am Skull13 the toning and chanting in the temples
- I Am Skull 13 the pipe organ in churches
- I Am Skull 13 the steady beat of the Shaman's drum
- I Am Skull 13 the healing rattle of the Medicine person
- I Am Skull13 the singing Crystal Bowls
- I Am Skull 13 the flutes of the World
- I Am Skull 13 the African drum
- I Am Skull 13 the Human Voice singing "Halleluiahs" and Lullabies
- I Am Skull13 the Sound of the Prayers
- I Am Skull 13 the Sounds of All Creatures Worldwide
- I Am Skull 13 speaking all languages
- I Am Skull 13 the Alpha and the Omega
- I Am Skull 13 of Pure Unconditional Love
- I Am Skull 13 of Love and Acceptance in my Heart and Soul for every living Being and Intelligence

"Ah Ha" and So It Is!

The Time is NOW!!!!!!!

INTERVIEW WITH WILLIAM "BILL" HOMANN, USA
With Marilee A. Snyder- Nieciak

The Actual Interview with Bill Homann and the Skull of Love was set up for Friday, May 13, 2011 at 10:30 a.m. The answers to my direct questions are in italics.

(It is my personal belief after working with these Skulls that the M-H Skull of Love is Skull 13. Skull 13 on the 13th is a 22/4 day, double transformation number of 2x11 and 2+2 = 4 the number for the Earth. The following is from our interview with Bill Homann.)

166

Anna Mitchell-Hedges found the Skull at Lubaantun in what is now Belize on her 17th birthday, January 1, 1924. At that time the Skull was given to the Mayan people of the area. These people cared for the Skull while the Mitchell-Hedges party continued excavating the site for another three years. In 1927, as they prepared to leave the Mayans gave the Skull to Mitchell-Hedges for safe keeping. And except for a couple of brief periods it was in their care – As if it was meant to be.

The Mitchell – Hedges Skull is the most mysterious artifact in the World. It relates to human brains and knowledge.

Sometime in 1993 or 1994, Anna came to live with Bill and stayed for three years. At which point she returned to England and then back to Canada.

In 2001, Anna was very sick with bronchial problems. Bill went to Canada to get her to bring her back to the States so he could care for her. She then started teaching him and connecting him to the Mayan Elders so he can work with the Skull in a Good Way.

For the next six years they worked together as student/teacher and beloved friends and on his birthday in 2007 Anna passed the Skull to Bill and transitioned to the other-side of the veil that same day. Recently, Bill stated that he knew in 1980 that the Skull would be his to guard and care for.

The Skull is completely connected to Bill as a part of himself and Anna is in constant communication from the other-side. The Spirit World is as real as the 3-D world we live in. Bill said that he is in a dream state when working with the Skull and Anna.

He has been taking the Skull of Love to Spiritual Sites around the world where it connects to the Earth, including the crystalline sand beaches of Northwest Indiana, once a part of Atlantis. He lived in Northwest Indiana with Anna. The Singing Sands are 90 percent quartz Crystal as with the Original 13 Singing Skulls.

THE TIME IS NOW!

He kept saying that just like the Skulls did in our writing sessions when bringing forth their information – Fascinating for me.

The April 11, 2011 Questions Are:

How did you meet Anna and the M-H Skull?

167

While he was in the Military Service in Panama and saw articles on the Crystal Skulls with the history on the wall while visiting a huge Octopus. The he went to visit the Isla de Tobago where he met an English lady who told him stories of Anna and her father Mitchell-Hedges. He was "hooked." He knew then that it was his destiny to meet Anna and the Skull.

How do you communicate with the M-H Skull of Love and how often?

With him all the time – they are in constant communication.

How do you communicate with Anna now that she is on the other side of the veil?

Through the Skull, the other dimensions are more real than 3-D.

Why did this work come to us, Marilee and Marlene?

Many were called, few answered. Now connected – It is a Karmic connection and the past is being brought forward. Because it called for people with special gifts to give insight.

What do you want us to know about the Skull that is Not a part of the Public Domain?

The real Essence of the Skull of Love is that it opens up the heart chakra – giving females full power with all the feminine gifts being brought forward. It opens everyone up to.

Universal Love – Balance of Duality.

The conch shell represents the spiral up with open energy to the Universal Energies. Right now, on Earth the Spiral is clogged. We need to return to the MIND of the HEART. All Life Forms are Connected. It is the Time of the Priestess in Harmony and Balance with the Priest.

Is it possible that the M-H Skull of Love is an ancient computer? Can it be accessed by the human bio-computer?

The M-H Skull is electropiezo crystal – the stuff of all computer chips, memory chips in cell phones and computers.

The M-H Skull is from Atlantis, which as a culture destroyed the Earth. Now we have to Heal the Earth.

It holds Universal Knowledge that can be accessed by the human heart and mind. It connects to the pineal gland – the electropiezo crystal in humans.

That is what you are doing in your work.

Are all of the Skulls "Healing Skulls" for humans, animals and all of the kingdoms of Nature including the microbial? Bill did not answer this question per se.

What do you want us to know about your work and purpose that is not on any website?

Our area in Northwest Indiana was Atlantis.

What personal experiences and adventures are you willing to share about with regard to Anna and the Skull?

They also worked with two other of the Original Skulls in the physical and he continues this work today.

How do you work with John of God?

John of God does Spiritual and Emotional Healing. Humans heal the Spiritual and Emotional bodies, must do this before heal the Physical body. Bill is a good friend and apprentice. He cares for him and works with him at the center. Go to http://www.JohnofGodcasa.com. There are two more casas, the one in Brazil and the one in Italy. Bill has hired someone to run the John of God Casa in Arizona. There is a Mother Crystal weighing 8500 pounds in the Arizona Casa that triangulates Energy with the sites in Brazil and Italy to bring up the vibrations of the area and for the entire Earth, to help the Earth.

The Skull needs to be protected so that the information is preserved. The M-H Skull is in a different location.

How does John of God work with the Mitchell-Hedges Skull? Does he work with any other Skulls?

He doesn't really work with the Skulls in his work. He is a Spiritualist that works with Entities and Planes of Existence.
What is the purpose of Hollows in the Skull?

Doesn't want to get into that now; not ready to talk about yet.

What is the purpose of the prisms and lens?

The prisms and Lens inside the Skull can only be produced in zero gravity. The Skull was found in Central America. It is NOT from Earth. Zero Gravity ONLY exists in Space.

Then Bill told us a story about how the Mayan Priests put a stone on a fire and put the Skull on the Stone. When removed Skull from stone, fire came out of the Skulls eyes. Then he said Truth is Truth.

Is the Mitchell-Hedges Skull androgynous?

The Skull is a Shape Shifter. It is both female and male.

Does the Mitchell-Hedges Skull have DNA codes and qualities?

Not sure, never thought about it. It is an Entity with a personality.

If so, what scientific studies have deciphered these codes?

Never done.

Are the original Skulls extra-terrestrial in nature?

The Mitchell-Hedges Skull is Extra-Terrestrial.

What are the past-life relationships, if any, for you and the Skull?

We have been together in many lifetimes - Atlantis, Egypt, Mayan and with major civilizations.

What previous connection do you, Anna, Marlene and Marilee have with M-H Skull?

Mayan is the highlight of where we all worked together Marilee was in Atlantis working in a different way with crystals and computers.

How do you receive from the M-H Skull?
Knowing; Feeling – some hear a voice.

170

What do you receive from the M-H Skull, healing, guidance, knowing, and energy/power?

All of this and more information.

How many dimensions does the M-H Skull access?

Center to Center; Top to Bottom. No one has been able to put a number to the dimensions.

Bill has his own name, not able to share.

What dimension does it prefer to work in?

Earth is where it is working now.

In our work we were told it is the Alpha and the Omega, Skull 0 and 13 of the Original 13   Skulls - The Skull of Love. Do you have a name for the Skull? See the answer below. It is zero and 13

What do you want us to call the M-H Skull, other than by its number 13?

By numbers is the best way. They don't have to have a name.

How does the M-H Skull work the other Original Skulls 1 to 12? –

See answer below in email

Is there any specific information that you can share that we will not get from the Akashic Records or Shamanic Journeys to the MH Skull?

Go with your Gut. (A personal note – with the crystal skulls, Akashic Records and shamanic   Journeys – we have access to all knowledge.)

What new information does the MH Skull want to bring forth that the other known Skulls do not have?

Love Light, as humanity changes open to greater knowledge. Relax and Let It Happen.

How can people meet the M-H Skull now?

The Skull has its own Energy Field that gives off positive energy. It soothes discordant Energies and gives Love. It Mirrors Inner Self – opens the log jam. People can learn to connect with its energies without being in the physical.

When will your Museum and Center open?

After all the final details are complete for the Casa for John of God he will start working on the Center.

What kind of Classes and Programs will your Center/Museum offer?

He talked about the pole shift of the Earth and how important it is to fill our entire being, especially the Mer-Ka-Ba. He is working with Drunvalo Melchizedek. Bill feels that Drunvalo's books "The Ancient Secret of the Flower of Life- Vol. 1 and 2" are the best spiritual writing available plus his book "Living from the Heart." He says someone needs to teach the expansion of the Mer-Ka-Ba in person. When the pole shifts occur if the individual's Mer-Ka-Ba isn't in place all our memories and knowledge held in our electrical fields will disappear. We will go back to pre-caveman. Learn to do the Mer-Ka-Ba work.

How can we support your work?

Fill our Heart with Love and open to new vibrations.

These questions were written on April 11, 2011. On April 12, 2011, early in the morning, I was awakened with the following message from the Mitchell-Hedges Skull saying:

I am the Alpha and Omega
I am the Center of the Circle and the Circle.
I am the Mayan Zero (0) and number 13 not number one.

There are 12 Skulls besides myself. We work together.

I am the Skull of Love and Embody all the attributes of Love and there are 13 main attributes not the 8 that you currently use.

So your question is - How Skulls 1 thru 12 and I work together?

We do work together - we are in constant communication with each other through telepathy and the Languages of Light and Sound depending on

172

which Skull is talking and the information being disseminated and for what purpose. Our realms are much more complicated and vaster than most humans can imagine and it is the intricacies that are communicated to maintain the Earth's Balance and bring open hearted Love to humans and all of their interactions with each other and all of Nature.

(A personal note - The distinct feeling was one of a very powerful female presence speaking directly to me in a very intimate way - as if we have known each other for forever. She was strong and comforting giving me the correct information as a Mother would her child - in a kind gentle way... It felt very loving and she said that more will be revealed when we work directly with her in our sessions - I can hardly wait.)

The Mitchell-Hedges Skull bi-locates and this is a perfect example of that ability.

This is an addendum to our original list of questions with The Skull. The corrections were made above for clarity. Also, I have the original full transcript of the Bill Homann interview.)

A Personal Note:

When we began this writing adventure, I cared for one Rose Quartz Skull that is called ROSE. Then Marlene brought a very small Sodalite crystal Skull I call BLUE ROSE and on Monday, August 20, 2012 my third Skull arrived from Gina. She is CYDONIA; a beautiful golden burnt orange Jasper. I now have a Crystal Skull family...I'm looking forward to working with Cydonia, who carries the energy of Athena and Mars. Since her arrival, I've been able to edit and complete this manuscript in four days. Amazing, as Cydonia is also helping with the healing of my left knee. Kirsten's book and cards arrived from Germany – so excited to be working with all of this fabulous energy.

On Halloween after a Drum Circle with the World Drum, journeying to the element of Air and the Winds of Change, I received a beautiful Chinese Fluorite Skull named MONA MARIE. On 12.12.12 I received a bone skull, STAR CHILD, from my neighbor. These Skulls all helped complete the e-book edition of this book on March 31, 2013.

Then in June of 2013, I bought a pair of Skulls – YIN and YANG perfectly balancing the Energies. Yin in a small Hematite Skull and Yang is a Clear Quartz Skull.

Then on August 3, 2013 my Crystal distributor, Gene Corn of Wolf Treasures, from our old store was in Niles, Michigan. I went to see him and bought six Skulls and some crystals and minerals. The minerals I purchased are black Kyanite, Indigo Gabbro, natural Azurite, green Obsidian and the crystals are a Record Keeper crystal point and a small Lemurian.

My six new Skulls are: Jade, named JADE; Purple Fluorite named GRATITUDE. These names came quickly. The other names came over the next eight days. After the names of the Skulls started coming is when I began the revision. It was as if they completed the energy so the re-vision could begin. The next Skull to reveal her name was Moss Agate, who is SEE-MOTHER as I photographed them. The pictures are in the back of grids and the Skulls in circles with different Centers anchored by Cydonia in the South and Yin and Yang in the North. As I was putting the pictures in the manuscript, Orange carnelian told me her name is CREATIVITY. As I continued the re-vision Sardonyx told me she is called EARTH and Blue Sodalite is SEA and as I write she added wind. Her name is SEA-WIND, Air and Water, West and East, Spring and Autumn. WOW!

PART III

ACCESSING YOUR PERSONAL POWER SKULL(S)

Please NOTE that in the Southern Hemisphere the North South positions are REVERSED relative to the Attributes of Each One – Summer South is Winter and Winter North is Summer.

Accessing the Skulls with the vibration of your personal numerology also came in bits and pieces over several weeks. This will give you insight into your Soul's lessons from the ancestors, your Karma and your destiny and how to achieve it, working with your personal year Skull. There are many layers and as you work with the Skulls you will experience clarity.

Accessing the Skulls with your Vibrations and Numerology is the beginning for people that don't access the Akashic Records or journey in the Shamanic way of direct revelation. There is much to be revealed to you using this method. This is a foundation step even for the most seasoned practitioner of the Records or Journeying.

Your Access the Original 13 Crystal Skulls Using Your Numerology:

Numerology and your vibrations based on your birth date and name will give you the frequencies in numbers to determine which Skulls to work with for Your Karma Issues, Your Physical/ Material Issues, Your Soul and Spiritual Issues, Your Destiny and for the unfolding of Your Possibilities.

The Mayan Cross, an equilateral cross, is your Medicine Wheel and reveals:

Personal Life Lessons,
What you brought with you

Personal Destiny
You are the center of the cross, the fifth point.

A more detailed description of each point on the Medicine Wheel follows

175

NORTH POINT - KARMA

Karma represents your birthday date and with your DNA, it represents the ancestral linage of previous lives and all the information in your genes from your parents that were imprinted at conception, which determines your birth date. This is the North Point on the Medicine Wheel

EAST POINT

The East Point on the Medicine Wheel is how you present yourself to the world. This is your Physical/ Material Side is determined by the letters in your birth name and will not change much with a married name attached.

WEST POINT

The West Point on the Medicine Wheel is your Spiritual/ Emotional Number based on the vowels in your birth name. This is your Spirit and Soul Number. If you change your name completely, East, West and Destiny numbers need to be re-done.

SOUTH POINT

The South Point on your Medicine Wheel is the sum of your numbers is your Destiny Number. It is the total of your Karma Number plus your Physical/ Material Number plus your Spiritual Emotional Number. This is where you aim your life for your growth on all levels.

CENTER POINT

The Center is for the year we live in. For example my husband turns 70 this year.

In the Center he will be working with Skull 7 in the West, Spiritual Emotional, plus all of the other Skulls based on his numbers. If you are 10, you will be working with Skulls 1 and 10. This number changes on your birthday. Someone 66 will work with Skulls 6, 12, 1 and 2. . This number is from birthday to birthday.

We will use an example of a person that I made up from a combination of family and friends. Our person is Emma Catherine Smith born on September 29, 1955.

Emma's Karma Number is:

$9 + 2\ 9 + 1955 = 9 + 29 = 38 + 1955 = 20 =$
$38 + 20 = 58 = 5 + 8 = 13/4\ (1+3 = 4)$
Emma's Karma Number is 13/4.

The Karma Number is 4 at the lowest vibration of Skull 4 moving to the highest vibration Skull 13, Love.

All numbers have a vibration and frequency. Therefore all letters have a corresponding number (vibration) and a numerical frequency. The chart below shows the English language letters with their numbers. Ultimately, we only use number 0 to 9. The larger numbers are reduced to correspond with the number of each Skull.

All letters have this numerical value:

A = 1   J = 10/1 S = 19/10/1
B = 2   K = 11/2   T = 20/2
C = 3   L = 12/3U = 21/3
D = 4   M = 13/4   V = 22/4
E = 5   N = 14/5   W = 23/5
F = 6   O = 15/6   X = 24/6
G = 7   P = 16/7Y = 25/7
H = 8   Q = 17/8   Z = 26/8
I = 9   R = 18/9

East Point (Physical/ Material Side) Number is the sum of all of the consonants in her name:

Emma Catherine Smith

M + M = 13/4 + 13/4 = 26/8 (Look at 2 and 6 as Foundation Numbers for 8)

C + T + H + R +N = 3 + 20/2 + 8 + 18/9 + 14/5 = 63/9 (NEED to Look at 3 and 6 as Foundation Numbers for 9)

S + M + T + H = 19/10/1 + 13/4 + 20/2 + 8 = 60/6

26/8 + 63/9 + 60/6 = 23/5 = The Sum of the Consonants = Physical/ Material Number of 5 for Skull 5 which sits in the East

Spirit/ Soul Number equal the sum of the vowels in her name:

Emma Catherine Smith – vowel numbers

E + A = 5 + 1 = 6

A + E + I + E = 1 + 5 + 9 + 5 = 20/2

I = 9 for Smith

6 + 20/2 + 9 = 35/8 =

The Sum of the Vowels is 8. The Spirit/Soul Number is 8 for Skull 8 which sits in the North

Emma Catherine Smith's Destiny Skull is the sum of her

Karma Number (13/4),
Spirit Number (35/8) and her
Physical Number = (23/5) =
13/4 + 35/8 + 14/5 = 62/8

Emma's Destiny Number is Skull 8. Emma's Karma Number, her Spirit Number and her Destiny Number are all an eight (8). Emma's primary Skull is Skull 8 because it showed up three times, Karma, Spirit and Destiny. The secondary Skull is Skull 5.

The Center Number is starts on September 28, 2012 (day before actual birthday) and continues for one year. On her birthday, Emma will be 57, 5 + 7 = 12. Skull 12 is the foundation theme for her work with Skull 8 and Skull 5.

The Center Number changes again on September 28, 2013 continuing for one year. It just so happens that Emma's age corresponds to the last two digits of the calendar year. On September 29, 2012, Emma will be 57 = 5 + 8 = 13. Skull 13 becomes the foundation theme with her work with Skull 8 and Skull 5.

On our Medicine Wheel with Skulls 1 to 13, the Center is Skull 13 of Love and that is the ideal to strive for. With the other Skulls in their appropriate place on the Medicine Wheel, interacting with each of the other Skulls, exchanging and sharing information and wisdom.

In your personal Mayan Cross, YOU are the Center, for you truly are your own Center. You bring forth your unique gifts as a part of the Unity Consciousness of Oneness. Your Center is where you shine Your Light into the world while being anchored deep into the Earth. As you work with your Skulls, go to the section in the book for your particular Skull. Your age is for the number for the Center Skull.

Our Emma goes to Skull 8 for Karma, Spirit and Destiny; Skull 5 for Physical Material information for dealing with the outer world.

Now you can do your own Mayan Cross Medicine Wheel. On the last page of Part XI – Pictures, we have included blank Mayan Cross page for you and your family and friends. You may print copies. Please include the artist's name so she receives the credit.

As you travel around your Wheel, if you work with each Skull individually, your vibrations will change. My vibrations changed so much that my Akashic Record Prayers changed twice in one year to higher vibration and frequencies.

This information is for you to play with. It is for you to enjoy as you delve deeper into who you are.

Emma is an example and her messages; three out of five are with Skull 8, then Skull 5 then the changing Skull in the center, which changes in September on her birthday. Yours changes on the day before your actual birthday.

Remember that each quadrant also has a corresponding color. Skull 13 is the Center and we used Pink and Green for Love and the Heart Chakra.

North is White = Skulls 4, 8 and 12
East is Red = Skulls 1, 5, and 9
South is Yellow = Skulls 2, 6, and 10
West is Black = Skulls 3, 7, and 11

CENTER = Skull 13 and You

Two different Medicine Wheels Follow:

The first one is easier to use in the Southern Hemisphere – Simply reverse Skulls 4, 8 and 12 with Skulls 2, 6 and 10.

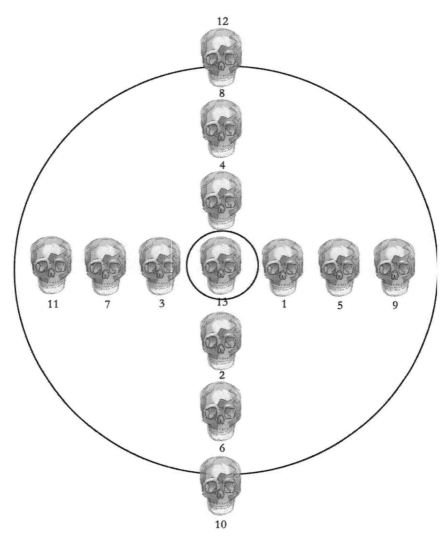

Saga-Oracle Art

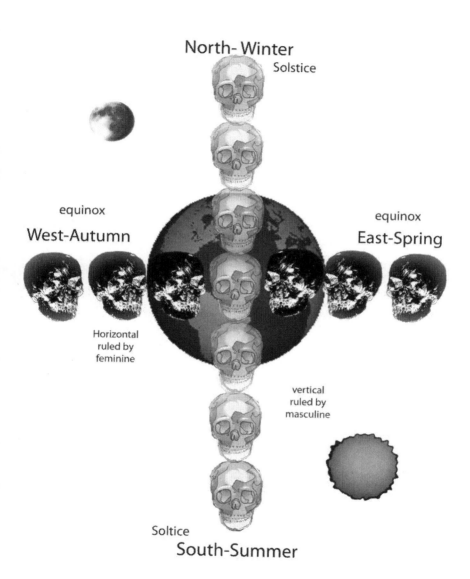

North-Winter
Solstice

equinox
West-Autumn

equinox
East-Spring

Horizontal
ruled by
feminine

vertical
ruled by
masculine

Soltice
South-Summer

PART IV

CAVES OF THE ANCESTORS ALIGNED WITH THE MEDICINE WHEEL

The Caves of the Ancestors each have their own Wisdom Wells. Caves traditionally are a place of Power where helping Spirits Dwell so Caves naturally assist in our Shamanic Journeys because our Ancestors and helping Spirits are waiting there to be of assistance with a Wisdom Well, which has morphed into an alter with a Crystal Skull on it with a circle of Elders around a fire waiting. No faces are visible. My personal experience is one of profound love, compassion and sharing. Listed below are the five caves with their attributes:

EAST = Cave of the Wind/Air which Moves Us

SOUTH = Cave of the Fire which Transforms Us (North below the Equator)

WEST = Cave of the Water which Shapes Us is in the West

NORTH = Cave of the Earth which Heals Us (South below Equator)

QUANTUM FIELD OF POSSIBILITIES = Cave of Crystal/Ether which Informs Us

The Stones, Bones and Crystals hold the Knowledge of All things

It was an eight month journey that I was guided to share with you, the Reader, and my experience is below.
It is why we need our stories.
It is what we need for stability in our lives.

Belonging:

In her writings, Maori Elder, Rose Perez, of New Zealand, explains basic concepts of her linage and culture; the Spiritual Songs and Ceremony that give structure to daily life. Billie Topa Tate, who founded the Mystical Science Institute in Evanston IL, also teaches these Spiritual Songs, Ceremony and Healing in the Apache Way, a matrilineal culture with deep roots, which is very rare in America. Rose and Billie know their Ancestors, do you?

Western Culture, whether Western Europe, Canada, North America, Australia, New Zealand, Tibet, or anywhere that has been invaded or famines or persecution of any kind, including lack of work, move to different countries to better their lives. Therefore, according to Paul Devereau, we are living in Nations of Immigrants, making us all displaced people. With rare exceptions, we do NOT know our ancestral roots, songs, stories or ceremonies.

This is my own amazing story in discovery of my ancestors. The 13 Crystal Skull led the way with Spirit... I discovered that pain in my left knee is my barometer. It hurts if I'm not following my Soul's lead. It all started at the Pebbles Retreat in March 2012 when we were told how to market "Pebbles". I did as suggested, all the while the pain in my knee got worse. I did an aggressive marketing campaign as suggested with drum circles and having classes.

Not realizing the impact of The Venus Transit and the Anchoring of the Divine Feminine Energy on the Summer Solstice and the Eclipses of May and June of 2012. I kept on doing drum circle book signings, Essential Oil Classes, my regular drum circles and experienced very deep and powerful Soul healings, with each one my knee got worse. This was my pattern for 40 days.

Finally after Lughnassah and the Full Moon Drum Circles of August on August 1 and 2, 2012 respectively I was hose bound. I could not stand on my left leg or walk. Asking "Why" in my own journeys I was told I didn't listen to my mantra "This is the old paradigm" – This is NOT the Feminine Way.

Finishing the original manuscript of this book *"Ancient Wisdom for Now – Crystals and The 13 Crystal Skulls"* became a priority along with Listening, Feeling and Receiving the messages of the Skulls and Spirit along with help from my husband and friends.

This went on for six weeks, learning to receive, be creative and trust my intuition, all attributes of the Sacred Feminine. During this time I was invited to participate in a Spirit Fest in Chicago with two of my original teachers from 20 years ago. I discovered a level playing field. During this same time, I was invited to participate in two Crystal Skull Conferences as a presenter. The first on-line conference in December, where I met fabulous new/old friends and one in Hot Springs, Arkansas, Oct 11,12,& 13, 2013. So exciting and I'm excited.

The World Drum was here from October 31, to November 4, 2012 for Ceremonies. Each one was for a direction or Element – that is when Ancestral Wisdom started to come through. A Grandfather/Elder in the Celtic Tradition and I received very similar answers from Spirit – The Beginning...

Then off to French Lick, IN for a retreat with my friend Juanita, where there was another Soul Retrieval to heal my deepest fear. This time it was my Mom as a little girl. My knee started hurting again. Once more I need to really retreat with my family to prepare for the Skulls on-line conference and "From Tears to Triumph" tele-lift.

Immediately after my presentation on *"How to Access Your Power Crystal Skulls"*, I received a phone asking me to host the Mitchell-Hedges Skull of Love on December 6, 2012. We gathered 11 people including the Skull guardian and myself for the opening evening of the Mayan Ceremonies. The Skull guided us to continue our ceremonies using the drum and journeys on 12.12.12; on the New Moon December 13; the Winter Solstice December 21, 2012 and on the Full Moon December 28, 2012. During this time I am to eat no red meat, stay quiet, and stay calm, pray daily with my drum for everyone, the Earth and the Universe and Be Love.

12.12.12 was the 40th Anniversary" of my "Death Experience." It is also the closing of the Celtic Year and eve of a new 26,000 year Era on the Mayan calendar. Change and transformation is happening personally, globally and in the cosmos.

Gandhi said *"Be the Change"* and I have been "the change' for the last 40 years. More changes started. As I read the Foundation for Shamanic Studies Annual *"Shamanism"* the article on Celtic Shamanism kept calling me then I received the card deck by John Matthews and Wil Kinghan for "Ancient Wisdom and Guidance". I was being guided by Spirit and the Skulls.

During this six month period, Mother Earth changed dramatically in my journeys to her.

June through December 6 she was covered from head to toe in a "bling" coving of diamonds set in platinum. I ask why and she said not enough people were shining their Light. Then on December 12, 2012 in our journey circle she morphed into a very young pregnant woman with NO bling. – I asked why – she told me that enough people were embracing their light and she didn't need the extra protection.

Following is our ceremony where for the first time we taken to our Cave, discovering which cave we were to work in for this Ceremony. I was in the Crystal Cave – Ether, The Quantum Field of Possibilities. The other Caves are the Cave of the Wind, The Cave of the Fire, The Cave of the Water and the Cave of the Earth. Corresponding Pictures are in Part X.

12.12.12 Ceremony:

Smudge
Call in Directions
Drum to Raise Vibrations
Giovanni's Prayer

Discussion Regarding Today – 12.12.12 Significance
Guided Meditation to Anchor in our Star Light

Drum - Three Journeys –
What can I do to Love myself more?
What can I do for Mother Earth?
How do I bring Love, Peace and Harmony to the Universe?

Discussion:

Shungo (Inca for My Heart To Your Heart) A closing I learned from "Ipu"

In the four and one half months since August 2, I have received a crystal skull family – one skull at a time. I had one that was un-named until Cydonia arrived, adopted Blue Rose, Mona Marie came on Halloween and Star Child came on 12.12.12. The project for 2013 is to get my book on the Ancient Crystal Skulls published. Now that it is published e-book as I finish the re-vision I have 13 crystal Skulls.

Miracles and Love for All... Be Love!

On the Winter Solstice we had a small quiet, sincere group where we breathed deeply did a Meditation. We Journeyed to Mother Earth asking

185

about the "Spirit of Newness" for her and for ourselves as we experience the Shift. This time she appeared slim, beautiful and radiant with a tiny New Earth in her left elbow. This is the first time we went down the Wisdom Well for our answers. WE didn't have a Full Moon Ceremony as guided because my brother-in-law passed that day.

On the New Moon Ceremony of January 11, 2013 new people showed up, it always exciting when "seekers" come to join our community... We Journeyed to our specific cave that wanted to work with us to manifest our Contentment. We all did releasing work before we could find our contentment. Mother Earth was changing again starting to gain weight as did her baby New Earth.

The very first time I met Mother Earth as my guide, she came as the Goddess of Willendorf. The very voluptuous "Great Goddess" and kept this shape until 12.12.12, when she began changing again and with each successive ceremony.

Eve of Imbolc/ Candlemas Ceremony was February 1, 2013 it is the day the old Woman goddess of Winter drinks from the Sacred Well and is transformed into the virgin Brigit.

For this ceremony I was guided to prepare Holy Water with Frankincense and Myrrh for washing of hands then anoint each person with Spikenard to amplify the Christ energy in each participant as an enlighten master Then we added the Crystal Skulls at the bottom of the Wisdom Wells. We worked with the Water, washing away what no longer serves to experience our Oneness, receiving wisdom.

On the New Moon, February 10, 2013 new people filled with fear showed up and not only did Mother Earth once gain cover herself in "Bling" I was also in an identical covering of diamond set in platinum. We barely got to the caves. We did not work with the wells.

Up until now, the New Moon of March 10, 2013, Spirit gave me guided meditations for the participants moving from a golden meadow, through the woods to white light where the answers were revealed when we met our guides and helpers on the opposite side of the white light threshold. This time I was guided to have our Souls lead the way and change how I called in the directions, casting the circle. Today's work was about planetary stewardship. The three journeys were:
What is planetary stewardship for my Soul?
What am I to do for planetary stewardship for the highest and best god of all?

What am I and my Soul to complete for Mercury Retrograde in preparation for the Vernal Equinox and Spring?

For the Equinox we went to the Cave of Wind/Air for New Beginning, New Communication, and New Growth. The Equinox is a day of balance with equal amounts of light and dark/day and night. This time there was another change the Skull was sitting on top of the Wisdom Well waiting. Our Journeys were:

What is my Balance?
What do I do to achieve my Balance?
What do I do to maintain my balance?

Mother Earth is back to looking like the great Goddess of Willendorf holding her child, The New Earth.

EACH OF THE 13 CRYSTAL SKULLS is a WISDOM WELL IN ALIGNMENT WITH THE CAVE OF ITS DIRECTION!

This is the Shamanic verbiage for these Libraries of Light along with the Shamanic Journeys that are the story of my 8 month odyssey from the Venus Transit to Now – embodying the Feminine, Listening in the Caves of the Ancestors and to the Wisdom Wells.

Will You Listen and Act of your Ancestors in the Caves and Your Soul's Guidance and that of the Wisdom Wells of the Original13 Skulls?

The Time Is NOW!

PART V

DEDICATION:
IPUPIARA MAKUNAIMAN AND HIS WIFE CLEICHA

This book is dedicated to Ipupiara Makunaiman (Dr. Bernardo D. Peixoto) is a shining light, who left the Earth plane on May 16, 2011. He will return to help us all. Let us rejoice in his teaching, wisdom, guidance and love...

"Ipu" and his wife were our house guests on two occasions for the Healing Waters Events just after September 11, 2001 and a year later, both at the time of the Autumn Equinox – A time of balance.

Bernie loved Lake Michigan with its 90 percent quartz crystal sand and a body of fresh water wider than the Amazon River. He was a beloved healer, teacher, mentor and friend to many including me, my husband and our community here in Northwest Indiana. He came to the USA to teach living from the heart in love with everything, especially the Earth.

Dr. Piexoto was an Anthropologist and worked at the Smithsonian and consulted with The National Zoo when we met him in 1999. He was a dedicated environmentalist, healer and teacher from the Ure-ewau-wau (People of the Stars) tribe of Brazil, the last shaman of his people (only 30 members of this tribe are still alive on Earth).

Dr. Peixoto was a co-founder of Dream Change Coalition with John Perkins. He founded The Native Cultural Alliance and Eco Global Journey, organizations dedicated to the preservation and sharing of native cultures and wisdom, especially in his beloved Brazil.

What Ipupiara taught me gave me the ability to share the wisdom of the Original 13 Crystal Skulls. He showed us how to use crystals on the bottoms of feet to heal and align. He also taught humor in all endeavors of life... His wife called him a "tricky" Shaman.

This dedication is not complete without mentioning Ipu's wife Cleicha, Jenny Zamora Piexoto. She wrote the following Mother's Day Poem for me the week before Ipu transitioned – I am grateful and humbled. As if a torch was being passed.

Thank You Cleicha for being the strength and power behind Ipu, the Voice.

Cleicha often laughed heartily at my husband John and me. Then one day she said: "Marilee, the wife is always the second Mother; it is your job to teach him."

Cleicha's poem is fitting for the Original 13 Crystal Skulls – The Mothers and Grandmothers of Ancient Wisdom coming forward.

The Time Is Now!

CLEICHA'S POEM:

Together we will honor our mothers,
And The Mother.
Together we will honor the magic
Of Motherhood.

Together we will honor our infinite lineage of ancestors and dependents,
Matter on Mother, Mater Earth.
Together we will have fond memories.
Together we will laugh.
Together we will cry.

All Mothers that provide us the everlasting joy of loving.

For we know that a mother's love is unlike any other ~
Never fading
Never faltering
Filled with passion
That is the hallmark of the Earth plane
Through anger, fear, sorrow...
And ecstatic joy in our hearts
Uplifting our spirit,
For a mother's love is deeper than any other
And is forever present
As a sweet fluttering in our souls.

PART VI

ACKNOWLEDGEMENTS

First and foremost, I acknowledge my husband, John for his unwavering support, for being my best friend and greatest teacher with his profound observations filled with humor. His editing help is priceless.

Thanks to the 13 Original Crystal Skulls; the Masters, Teachers and Loved Ones; my Helpers and Guides who assisted and contributed so much. Thanks to the Original 13 Skulls for calling me to grow, transmute and transform... A truly healing journey this, as it is ongoing.

To my dear friend Marlene Sanford Rhodes, who was instrumental in getting the book started, something I had been avoiding. Thank you for being my writing companion as we toured the Records and journeyed for five months. Your support made this book possible. You are so very much appreciated; my heart is filled with love, appreciation and gratitude for you.

Thank you to Master Bill Homann, who took the time to answer our questions in our first interview. Gratitude fills my heart for the pictures of Skull of Love at sacred sites. He encouraged the writing of this information from our first conversation. I so appreciate his trust in me and my work.

Much appreciation and thanks to Gina O'Connor and Kristen Hilling for their interviews, insight and their generosity sharing themselves and their Skulls. Such loving Souls that helped introduce me to a community that practices Love and all of its attributes. To Joshua Shapiro who joined our group of Skull caregivers in August of 2012 when the 13 Skulls suggested I contact him. Lastly, to my friend, Linda (Allayah) Frisch, thank you for her contribution. I met her through Joshua's first On-line Crystal Skull Conference as a co-presenter. My heart overflows with Gratitude to the five Skull caregivers who also provided pictures of their Skulls, thank you.

Paula Rosenfeld for all of the Soul Retrievals and Guidance that she provided over the course of the first six months of this project so I could continue to write and enter the writing contests. Thanks and appreciation to my many personal teachers mentioned throughout the book.

Huge thanks to Christine Kloser, her Transformational Author Experience and for awarding me a chapter in her Anthology "Pebbles in the Pond – Transforming the World One Person at a Time." She called together Soul families that met at the Pebbles Retreat in Maryland.

There are no words to express my Love and Gratitude to Each Soul Sister and Brother that contributed to my stepping out into the fullness of who I Am. You know who you are, my Soul Family. Such magic and miracles have occurred by our living in the next paradigm. Each of these wonderful people is an Agent for Change, a Transformer bringing Balance and Harmony to individuals and the Earth.

My Deep Gratitude to Kathy Jennings; I appreciate for her editing and Kimberly Burnham for her help with the cover and getting the Kindle e-book published. To Diane Nelson for jumping at the last minute to help with the print version cover, formatting and getting the book printed.

To you, the Reader, Thank You, with Deep Appreciation and Gratitude for your being called to experience the 13 Crystal Skulls and be a part of my life, I Love You and I Thank You.

NOW! The Time is NOW!

PART VII

BIBLIOGRAPHY

<u>Aeoliah</u> – Awakening Your Inner Light, Helios Rising Publishing, 1992 Emotional Healing of Self Abuse

<u>Barrios, Carlos</u> – The Book of Destiny, Unlocking the Secrets of the Ancient Mayans and the Prophesy of 2012 – Harper One 2009 – English Translation from Spanish by Lisa Carter

<u>Bourgault, Luc:</u> The American Indian Secrets of Crystal Healing, Quantum, an imprint of W. Foulsham & Co, Ltd. Capital Point, Slough, Berkshire, England - English Edition 1997

<u>Braden, Gregg</u> – The God Code – Secret of Our Past, the Promise of Our Future – Hay House Publishing - 2004

<u>Buchanan, Rev. Douglas V., DVD</u> – Ancient Wisdom from Dar'Shem material; Park Forest, IL 60466 http://www.gatesofhorn.com (crossed over June 21, 2011)

<u>Calleman, Carl Johann</u> – http://www.calleman.com/content/articles/the_tortuguero%20_monument.htm

<u>Cannon, Dolores:</u> The Three Waves of Volunteers and The New Earth, Ozark Mountain Publishing, Huntsville, AR 72740 copyright 2011

<u>Clow, Barbara Hand:</u>
Alchemy of the Nine Dimensions 2011/2012 Prophesies and the Nine Dimensions of Consciousness with Gerry Clow, Hampton Roads Publishing Company – 2004

The Mayan Code – Time Acceleration and Awakening the World Mind, Bear and Company – 2007

<u>Estes PhD, Clarrisa Pinkola:</u> UNTIE THE STRONG WOMAN: Blessed Mother's immaculate love for the wild soul. Sounds True, Inc., Boulder, CO 80306 2011

<u>Grattan, Brian</u> – Mahatma I and II – The I AM Presence – Light Technology Publishing, Sedona, AZ – 1994

<u>Homann, Bill</u> – www.MitchellHedges.com He gave us an Interview and he provided some of his personal photos of the Mitchell-Hedges Skull for the book.

Ingerman, Sandra – Shamanic Journeying – A Beginners Guide with Drumming CD (used for our Journeys) – Sounds True, Inc. – 2004

Ingerman, Sandra and Wesselman, Hank – Awakening To The Spirit World, The Shamanic Path of Direct Revelation, Sounds True, Inc. 2010

Javane, Faith and Dusty Bunker – Numerology and The Divine Triangle – Whitford Press, a division of Schiffer Publishing, Ltd. 1979 and Illustrations 1980

Kryder, Rowena Pattee: DESTINY Gaia Matrix Oracle Numerology, Golden Point, 1995

Matthews, John and Kinghan, Wil: The Shaman's Dream Oracle, Watkins Publishing, London 2012 – Text by John Matthews and Original Art by Wil Kinghan both in 2010 and 2012

Melchizedek, Drunvalo: "Living In the Heart" 2003, "The Serpent of Light" and "The Ancient Secret of the Flower of Life, Volumes I and II" – Light Technology Publishing, Flagstaff, AZ

Melody: Love Is In the Earth – A Kaleidoscope of Crystals Update – Earth-Love Publishing House, Wheat Ridge, Colorado 80033 USA – Third Printing 1995

Morton, Chris and Ceri Louise Thomas: 1997, 1998 and 2002 - "The Mystery of the Crystal Skulls – Unlocking the Secrets of the Past, Present and Future, Bear & Company, Rochester, Vermont

Mykian, W, - Numerology Made Easy, Wilshire Book Company, 1979

Parry, Dannan: The Essene Book of Days 2001, Earthstewards Network Publishing 2000, Bainbridge, WA, USA

Redfield, James – The Twelfth Insight – The Hours of Decision – Grand Central Publishing, 2011

Sams, Jamie: The Thirteen Original Grandmothers, copyright 1992

Scallion, Liz,
http://www.soundsofsirius.com/crystal_skulls_mitchell_hedges.html_-
Sounds of Sirius Crystal Skull - which is preparing us for that quantum leap...
It's believed that some of the original 13 skulls of ... I believe that the Crystal Skulls are agents for healing and teachers of...
www.soundsofsirius.com/crystalskulls.html

The Saga-Oracle: (Iva Deane Gemmell) Jeshua's Song, copyright 2011, Infinity Publishing, West Conshohocken, PA 19428-2713

Twist, Lynne – The Soul of Money – Reclaiming the Wealth of Our Inner Resources – W.W. Norton & Company -2003 with Teresa Barker

PART VIII

RESOURCES

First, we recommend all of the books in the bibliography. Of particular interest are the books and Resources listed below:

Barrios, Carlos – The Book of Destiny, Unlocking the Secrets of the Ancient Mayans and the Prophesy of 2012 – Harper One 2009 – English Translation from Spanish by Lisa Carter

Burnham, Kimberly: Theburnhamreview@juno.com for publishing coaching and cover design, West Hartford, CN

Calleman, Carl Johann –
http://www.calleman.com/content/articles/the_tortuguero%20_monument.htm

Gemmell, Iva Deane – Niles, MI, and USA Deane can be reached at www.facebook.com/Deane.Gemmel and www.facebook.com/Jeshua's Song she is known as the Saga-Oracle who does profound readings and channelings. She did the art work for the Medicine Wheels and she is mentioned in the Legends portion of this book. She is the author of "Jeshua's Song" and co-author of "Magdalene's Well".

Hilling, Kirsten: Germany Kirsten@horus-mystery-school.com and http://www.horus-mystery-school.com
Kirsten is the author of: "Crystal Skull Deck" – 44 cards with channeled Crystal Skull Messages with a Guidebook printed in English and German - ISBN 9 –783934–063709 by elraanis Publishing Germany. Gina, Bart and Allayah contributed to this book "Crystal Skulls – A Journey of Experience, Wisdom and the Divine" This is an anthology of the experiences of various Crystal Skull Guardians and Caretakers.

Homann, Bill – USA and the world www.MitchellHedges.com He gave us an Interview and he provided some of his personal photos of the Mitchell-Hedges Skull for the book.

International Spiritual Experience, Venlo, Netherlands, Gina O'Connor, Director www.ISE.org and www.facebook.com/ISE.org
Gina O'Connor: treeoc3@hotmail.com
Gina is the caretaker of many, many Crystal Skulls and helps them find homes. She works closely with Master carvers is China and Brazil. I received my Cydonia because of Gina and I am grateful. She posts beautiful pictures of all sizes and colors of Crystal Skulls looking for homes.
Gina was helped organize the Second Annual Crystal Skull Convention in Hot Springs, AR, USA. More information is listed below for this convention with the dates for 2013.
Through International Spiritual Experiences she organizes events around the world and works closely with Bart Peters.

Jennings, Kathleen: (Kathy) Book Editing ekathleen28@gmail.com, Kalamazoo, MI

Peters, Bart: Venlo, Netherlands www.luminousenergies.com and www.luminouesenergies.nl
http://www.shamanism.org/Leonidas@luminousenergies.com Bart is also known as Leonidas. He works closely with Gina O'Connor. He is an energy worker, manifesting and facilitator of energies with ceremonies, workshops and healings incorporating Sacred Sounds. He works with and is the caretaker of several, very old, Mongolian Crystal Skulls. He and Gina were on the Bob Charles blog talk radio show and Bart did a wonderful visual/musical Skull presentation...

Linda (Allaya) Frisch: New Jersey, USA. Linda is well known in the Crystal Skull Community and Loves sharing her Skulls, their Knowledge and Wisdom. She can be reached on facebook at www.facebook.com/Allayah and at these websites: www.sanctuaryoftheancients.com and a Circle of Hearts on facebook and www.CreatingCalmNetwork.com I met her through the First On-line Crystal Skull Conference and we became friends as if we had known each other in many life times, Soul family.

Joshua Shapiro and Katrina Head of Renton, WA, USA www.crystalskullexplorers.com -The Crystal Skull Explorers have been together since 2009. The Crystal Skull Explorers offer a free e-book, a free online newsletter called "The Unfolding of the Crystal Skulls" and do a periodic online radio show. Through their connecting with ATW (Awakening Truth Worldwide) they also offer online classes and are working on an online crystal skull conference. To explore these free treasure to the public please visit:
http://www.crystalskullexplorers.com/crystal-skulls.html

Paula Rosenfeld Chicago, IL, USA - With 20 years as my Shaman for Soul Retrieval, Extraction, Certified Intrinsic Coach®, Healer, Akashic Records, Clairvoyant Reader and leading Shamanic Journey Circles. Her website is: www.fromtheheartcenter.com or email, paula@fromtheheartcenter.com,

Crystals and Crystal Skull Convention - Hot Springs 3rd Annual Crystal and Crystal Skull Convention – October 11, 12 and 13, 2013, Little White Hawk Johnson (Cheryl Johnson) at 1-479 – 221-8176, Email - Cheryl Johnson - littlewhitehawk@hotmail.com
http://www.facebook.com/HotSprings2ndAnnualCrystal&CrystalSkullConvention

Foundation for Shamanic Studies - www.shamanism.org

Shamans Portal - http://www.shamanportal.org/

Alex Strangius, Alexstrangius@gmail.com

PART IX

AUTHOR INFORMATION

Rev. Marilee Ann Snyder- Nieciak, BSc,
Internationally Recognized Shamanic Practitioner, Transformational Author
and Crystal Skull Guardian

Rev. Marilee is a "Wounded Healer/Shaman" returned from the other side to
love and accept you as your healer, Spiritual guide and teacher, specializing
in Soul Retrieval and Restoration; Vibrational Healing Modalities and Young
Living Essential Oils.

Marilee is also a published author in the anthology *"Pebbles in The Pond –
Transforming the World One Person at a Time"* launched in May of 2012.
She is also in another Anthology called from *"Tears to Triumph Stories to
Transform Your Life Today"*

March 31, 2013 Sunday is the launch day my radio show "Soulful Sunday –
Ancient Wisdom for NOW!" launches at 9:30am Central time on
www.CreatingCalmNetwork.com I will be sharing more information,

knowledge and wisdom of our Souls and Crystal Skulls and their Legends on Soulful Sunday for 15 to 20 minutes. You can find the links on facebook.

On August 1, 2013, Marilee launched her television show "Ancient Wisdom for NOW on Creating Calm Network with Ann White Producer.

"Ancient Wisdom for NOW" is Marilee's third book and available in April of 2013; this book to be followed by *"Ancient Wisdom for NOW –Prayer and Guided Meditations"* in the Autumn of 2013. *"Ancient Wisdom for NOW – Healing Naturally with Shamanism and Creator's Gift, Pure Therapeutic Grade Essential Oils"*

Marilee is available for private appointments or to share her wisdom with presentations, drum circles and classes for you and your groups as well as individual healing and counseling sessions.

Watch for her and others in the documentary film *The Soul Shift Project,* Meghan Ross, Producer *and* You can find Marilee on these sites:

http://www.marileeasnyder.com AND
http://www.ancientwisdomforNOW.com
http://www.SageSpiritTerra.org;
http://www.linkedin.com/in/marileeasnyder;
http://www.facebook.com/MarileeASnyder-Nieciak;
www.facebook.com/ANCIENTWISDOMforNOW
www.PINTEREST.COM/MARILEESNYDERNI

Please join our mailing list by going to www.sagespiritterra.org or Sage Spirit Terra on Facebook.

PART X:

CRYSTAL SKULL PICTURES

FIGURE 1
MY GENERATOR CRYSTAL GRID

FIGURE 2
MY 13 CRYSTAL SKULLS, GRIDS WITH MY AMBER TURTLE

FIGURE 3
MY 13 CRYSTAL SKULLS WITH GENERATOR CRYSTAL CENTER

FIGURE 4
SOUL MUSIC OG SOUND AND LIGHT FREQUENCIES

FIGURE 5
MY CRYSTAL SKULL WITH CRYSTAL OWL GRID

FIGURE 6
MY NEW CRYSTALS & 6 SKULLS

FIGURE 7
MY SACRED ART ON A SUN DANCE BUFFALO SKULL GIFT

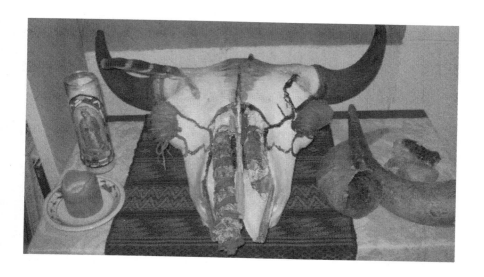

FIGURE 8
PLUTONIC SOLIDS FOR ANCIENT WISDOM FOR NOW

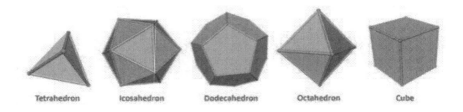

FIGURE 9
CELTIC MEDALION

FIGURE 10
MAYAN MEDICINE WHEEL

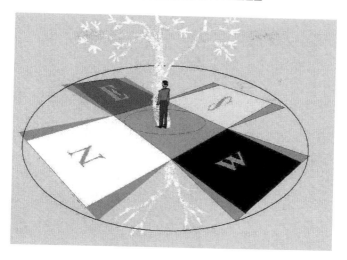

FIGURE 11
6 POINTED- STAR WITH COLORS

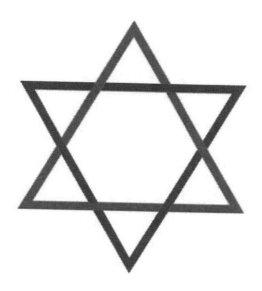

205

FIGURE 12
PLATONIC SOLIDS - THE ELEMENTS - THE SPINE

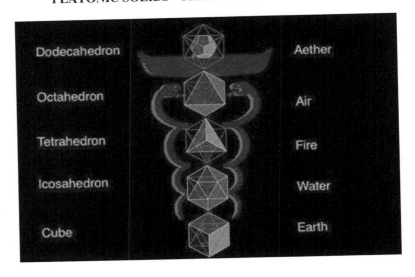

FIGURE 13
MY CHEVRON AMYTHEST

FIGURE 14
MY MOLDIVITE NUGGET

FIGURE 15
12.6.12 CEREMONY BILL HOMANN WITH THE M-H SKULL OF LOVE

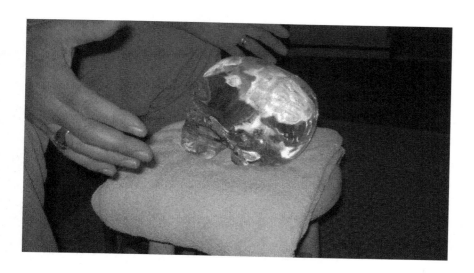

FIGURE 16
GINA O'CONNOR'S CALCITE MONGOLIAN - LEONID REGULUS

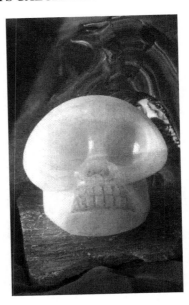

FIGURE 17
GINA O'CONNOR'S BRAZILIAN SKULL LIGHTWORKER

FIGURE 18
JOSHUA SHAPIRO'S SKULL PORTAL DE LUZ

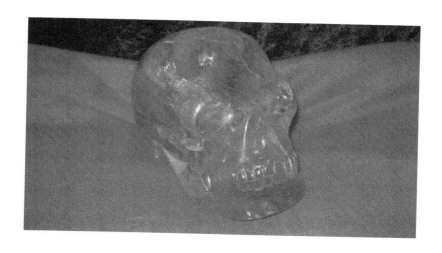

FIGURE 19
ALLAYAH'S SKULLS - WHITE TARA, WHITE DOVE,
MELCHIZEDEK, YAHWEH

FIGURE 20
KASPER - BY SVEN GROLICH BY KIRSTEN HILLING

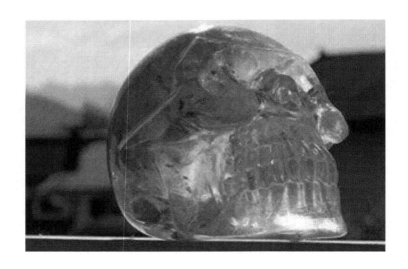

FIGURE 21
MY CRYSTAL SKULL CYDONIA

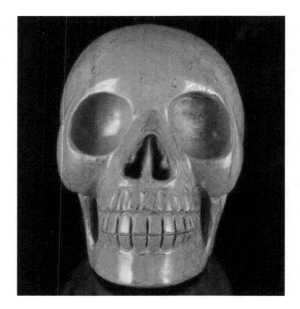

FIGURE 22
MY NEW CRYSTAL SKULL DESK ALTAR

FIGURE 23
MY RECORD KEEPER, GENERATOR, LEMURIA AND
PHANTOM CRYSTAL GRID

FIGURE 24
12.6.12 CEREMONY THE SAGA-ORACLE/DEANE GEMMELL WITH
THE M-H SKULL OF LOVE

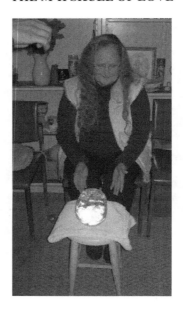

FIGURE 25
12.6.12 CEREMONY WITH THE M-H SKULL OF LOVE

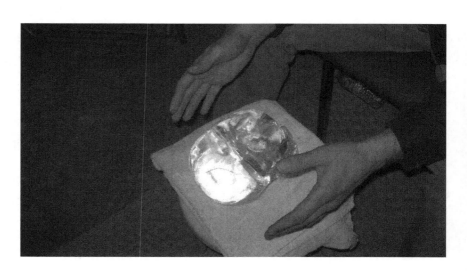

FIGURE 26
12.6.12 CEREMONY WITH THE M-H SKULL OF LOVE

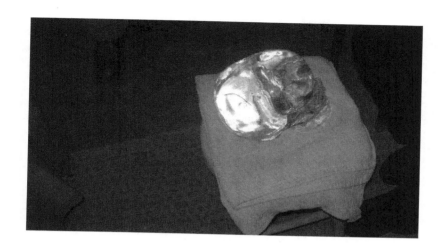

FIGURE 27
12.6.12 CEREMONY ME WITH THE M-H SKULL OF LOVE

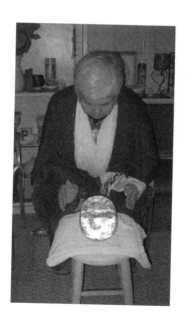

FIGURE 28
12.6.12 CEREMONY WITH THE M-H SKULL OF LOVE

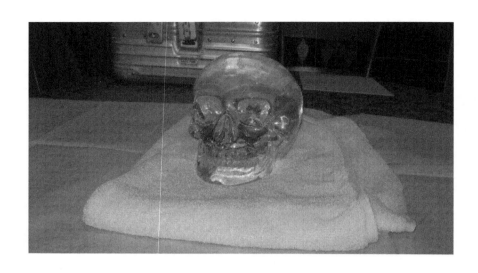

FIGURE 29
12.6.12 CEREMONY WITH THE M-H SKULL OF LOVE

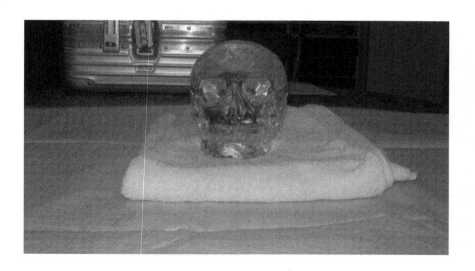

FIGURE 30
SKULL CROSS GRAPHIC for ACCESSING YOUR POWER SKULL

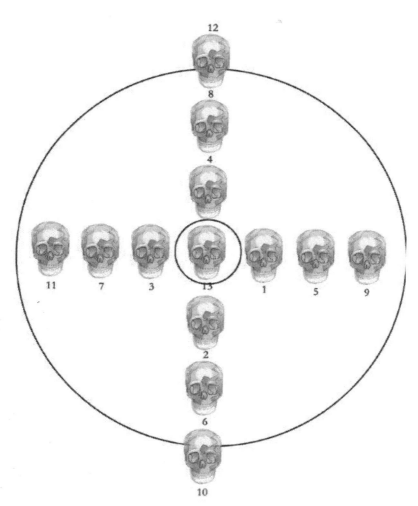

Saga-Oracle Art

FIGURE 31
ANCIENT WISDOM FOR NOW LOGO

66458873R00124

Made in the USA
Columbia, SC
21 July 2019